"The most thorough 'how-to' I've seen for getting your script out there and sold. The new chapter on using the Internet to promote your work is spot on."

— Scott Rice, award-winning short film writer/director, *Script Cops*

"Kathie Fong Yoneda knows the business of show from every angle and she generously shares her truly comprehensive knowledge — her chapter on the Web and new media is what people need to know! She speaks with the authority of one who's been there, done that, and gone on to put it all down on paper. A true insider's view."

— Ellen Sandler, former co-executive producer of *Everybody Loves Raymond* and author of *The TV Writer's Workbook*

"In this fast-paced, ever-changing world of multi-platform online content, finding a clear and concise voice to assist in navigating the landscape is an adventure in itself. In the second edition of *The Script-Selling Game*, Kathie Fong Yoneda provides her clear and concise insight on how to be successful in this 'wild, wild west' scenario. I highly recommend this book — it's a must-read for anyone who falls in the 'consumer-created content' file."

— L.A. Scheer, Media Goddess/Film & Broadcast Faculty, Tribeca Flashpoint Academy of Media Arts

"I've been writing screenplays for over 20 years. I thought I knew it all — until I read *The Script-Selling Game*. The information in Kathie Fong Yoneda's fluid and fun book really enlightened me. It's an invaluable resource for any serious screenwriter."

— Michael Ajakwe Jr., Emmy-winning TV producer (*Talk Soup*), executive director of Los Angeles Web Series Festival (LAWEBFEST), and creator/writer/director of *Who… and Africabby* (*AjakweTV.com*)

"Most screenwriters ask the same question: 'But how do I sell my script?' You begin by reading Kathie Fong Yoneda's book. It's thorough, essential, invaluable, and necessary. Kathie is an insider. She knows how the business works, how buyers think, and what writers have to know to get the script sold. Her insightful, encouraging style makes the impossible seem possible!"

— Dr. Linda Seger, author of *Making a Good Script Great, And The Best Screenplay Goes To…*, and *Writing Subtext*

"*The Script-Selling Game* is your own special insider's Fodor's, Lonely Planet, GPS and Yelp! guide to the exotic, exciting, sometimes confusing, sometimes dangerous, yet ultimately rewarding territory of Hollywood script sales. Kathie Fong Yoneda has not only explored this territory, she has actually carved out, tamed, and settled a lot of it in her years as a studio exec and as a producer. Her expertise in the special jargon, the specific tools, and the appropriate approaches will help you craft an effective presentation of your unique creative project, be it a feature film, a TV series, animation, game, web series or any other media production… Follow her guidelines, learn to speak the language, do the currency exchange from creativity-to-commerciality, and watch the barriers go down and the doors open up for you."

— Pamela Jaye Smith, workshop leader, writer, author of *Inner Drives, The Power of the Dark Side*, and *Symbols, Images, and*

"Having worked as an executive for most of the major studios, Kathie brings a rare insider's knowledge as she shares her behind-the-scenes information on developing your screenplay and marketing it – including the exciting new market of the Internet."

> — Pamela Wallace, writer/producer and Academy Award-winning co-writer of *Witness*

"Systematic, concise, real-world: three totally correct descriptions of Kathie Fong Yoneda's wonderful second edition of *The Script-Selling Game*. For myself, my graduate students, and my WGA professional screenwriting friends, this book best rings the selling bell. There are over thirty selling books on the Writers Store shelves. *The Script-Selling Game* is, by far, the most professional and accurate. A must-have if you want to get that terrific script of yours sold."

> — Lew Hunter, former chair of UCLA's screenwriting department, founder of the Indian Summer Screenwriting Colony, and author of *Lew Hunter's Screenwriting 434*

"Kathie Fong Yoneda wants you to succeed! In this updated version of *The Script-Selling Game*, she shares with you everything you'll need to know to succeed in the current marketplace. Of particular interest to animators will be the invaluable new chapter addressing that burgeoning field."

> — Kim Adelman, author of *Making It Big In Shorts*

"Kathie Fong Yoneda's done it again! This new edition of *The Script-Selling Game* provides important information regarding two very important components of the filmmaking world today: Animation venues, and using the Internet to your advantage. With her solid background in the film world, you definitely want to pay attention to what Kathie has to say."

> — Sable Jak, award-winning audio playwright and author of *Writing The Fantasy Film*

"Becoming a successful screenwriter means more than learning structure, character, and dialogue. Screenwriting is a business as well as an art. And no one tells you more about that business today than Kathie in her book, *The Script-Selling Game*. Buy it. Read it. And you'll be able to walk into any room in Hollywood and have that part covered."

> — Drew Yanno, screenwriting professor, consultant, and author of *The Third Act – Writing A Great Ending To Your Screenplay*

"Kathie Fong Yoneda, former studio exec, is launching her second edition of *The Script-Selling Game*. As a professional producer and screenwriter, I know the importance of listening to other pros in this crazy business. The new edition offers needed advice in such areas as animation and how to use the Internet to market your scripts. Well-done, Kathie!"

> — Catherine Ann Jones, author of *The Way of Story: The Craft & Soul of Writing*, Emmy-nominated writer/producer of *The Christmas Wife*, and staff writer on *Touched By An Angel*

"I didn't think *The Script-Selling Game* could be improved upon, but the second edition offers even more valuable information. I not only found the book to be practical with 'inside' information, but I now have a lot more knowledge about the Internet and animation — two subjects that are necessary and important for the 21st century scriptwriter. Whether you are starting your first script or have written several, read this book — it's a real treasure and I recommend it to all serious screenwriters."

> — Dr. Rachel Ballon, international script consultant, licensed psychotherapist, teacher, author of five writing books, including her latest, *The Writer's Portable Therapist: 25 Sessions To A Creativity Cure*

"If they gave Oscars for books on screenwriting, this book should be a serious contender!"

> — Signe Olynyk, writer/producer *Below Zero*, founder of The Great American PitchFest

"The new edition of *The Script-Selling Game* is, if possible, an even more invaluable resource for screenwriters than the first edition of the book. In this edition, Kathie Fong Yoneda delves into such critical topics as writing a query letter; the special considerations of submitting to TV; and the differences between a spec/reading script and a shooting script. She also includes brand new chapters on animation writing and how to utilize the Internet as a script-selling ally. I highly recommend this book to all writers who want to successfully navigate the Hollywood system and sell their screenplays."

> — Carolyn Handler Miller, author of *Digital Storytelling, Second Edition, A Creator's Guide to Interactive Entertainment*

"*The Script-Selling Game* is the new staple "must have" book for any writer wanting to succeed in television and film. What makes it stand out is the executive perspective from author/veteran Kathie Fong Yoneda. Kathie tells you everything you need to do, as well as what you should not do. If you want to sell your script and go through the transformation of being a writer to becoming a working writer, it's all here."

> — Jen Grisanti, story consultant, writing instructor for NBC WOTV, and author of *Story Line: Finding Gold In Your Life Story*

"Once again, Kathie Fong Yoneda draws on her wide experience of how the movie and TV game works, sharing the secret language and inner processes of the biz. It's a great timesaver for newbies, and a terrific review of the system for more experienced writers. It cleared up a lot of things for me, and you're sure to find useful insider information, especially in the new chapters on animation and writing for the Internet."

> — Christopher Vogler, story consultant and author of *The Writer's Journey*

"If you want to succeed as a Hollywood screenwriter, you have two choices: climb a tall mountain and ask an old bearded man to reveal his secrets, or read Kathie Fong Yoneda's new edition of *The Script-Selling Game*. Which will it be?"

> — Paula Berinstein, writer, instructor, founder of *The Writing Show*, and author of *The Writing Show* e-books

"If you're smart, you'll devour this book. It's like having your own personal industry guru to guide you through the realities and possibilities of script selling. *The Script-Selling Game* is a must-have for learning the ropes! Kathie is the real deal, and has been instrumental in helping me in my successful career in entertainment. Buy this book and take your first step on the path toward Hollywood."

> — Deborah Todd, writer, transmedia producer – *101 Dalmations: Escape From DeVil Manor, Curious George Comes Home, Blues Clues 1-2-3,* and author of *Game Design: From Blue Sky to Green Light*

"Kathie Fong Yoneda's book *The Script-Selling Game* is a necessary guide for any writer who wants to know how *it really is* in the world of pitching, developing and selling a screenplay. The second edition updates, focusing on animation and Internet distribution, empowering writers to expand their writing horizons and be creative with their careers."

> — Pilar Alessandra, screenwriting instructor, author of *The Coffee Break Screenwriter*

"This concisely-written, enthusiastic book steps away from the mere principles and philosophies of screenwriting to give its readers the much-needed practicalities of working in Hollywood and beyond. An absolutely invaluable addition to the market."

> — Dr. Craig Batty, Bournemouth University, UK, co-author of *Writing For the Screen: Creative and Critical Approaches*

"Pitching is one of the most intangible, nuanced, and daunting skills to master. But here, Kathie Fong Yoneda breaks it down into its simplest basics, giving beginners a chance to shave years off their training or development and leap ahead of their competition."

> — Chad Gervich, writer/producer: *Wipeout, Speeders, Foody Call, Reality Binge*; author of *Small Screen, Big Picture: A Writer's Guide to the TV Business*

"With new chapters on animation in film, television writing, and how the take-off of the Internet has launched new opportunities for writers, this is an up-to-date book that is worth a writer's time to read."

> — Erin Corrado, *onemoviefiveviews.com*

THE SCRIPT-SELLING GAME

A HOLLYWOOD INSIDER'S LOOK
AT GETTING YOUR SCRIPT SOLD
AND PRODUCED

SECOND EDITION

KATHIE FONG YONEDA

Published by
Michael Wiese Productions
12400 Ventura Blvd. #1111
Studio City, CA 91604
tel. 818.379.8799
fax 818.986.3408
mw@mwp.com
www.mwp.com

Cover Design: Johnny Ink *www.johnnyink.com*
Interior Book Design: Gina Mansfield Design

Printed by McNaughton & Gunn, Inc.,
Saline, Michigan
Manufactured in the United States of America

Library of Congress Cataloging-in-Publication Data

Yoneda, Kathie Fong
 The script-selling game : a Hollywood insider's look at getting your
script sold and produced / Kathie Fong Yoneda. -- [2nd ed.].
     p. cm.
 ISBN 978-1-932907-91-9
1. Motion picture authorship. 2. Hollywood (Los Angeles, Calif.) I.
Title.
 PN1996.Y58 2011
 808.2'30688--dc22
                                        2011002512

Mixed Sources
Product group from well-managed
forests and other controlled sources
www.fsc.org Cert no. SW-COC-002283
© 1996 Forest Stewardship Council
FSC

Amazon NBRS

To Denny,
whose unconditional love and patience
still amazes and inspires me!
. . . .

Table of Contents

Preface

by Pamela Wallace

I've been extremely fortunate to have Kathie Fong Yoneda's insightful advice and constructive criticism on nearly every screenplay I've written. She is a valued mentor to me. Now she can be your mentor as well through this ultimate insider's guide to writing, marketing and selling your screenplay.

Kathie has been a story analyst/development executive with an impressive background in the film and television business. Story analysts are usually the first to read your script and either recommend it to the people in a position to buy it or "pass" on it. Kathie's creative and commercial judgment has been honed by years of working in the trenches at most of the major studios. In this book, she gives you the hard-won wisdom, advice and critical information that only someone with her experience could possess.

The message of Kathie's first book was "Here's what you need to know to sell your script, from the viewpoint of someone who truly knows what she's talking about." That message is even more true in this updated, revised edition. There is new information on current movies, as well as submitting to television. Most exciting of all, there is a whole new section on using the rapidly changing world of new technologies to market and even produce your script on the Internet. This is a resource that can be particularly helpful to those of you who live outside of Hollywood.

You'll learn how to develop your initial movie idea. But that's just the beginning. Then comes the *really* hard part that stymies most writers: How to navigate the long and challenging process of marketing your script. This includes both traditional markets like studios and production companies, and now exciting new opportunities on the Internet. There are resources online that didn't exist just a few short years ago.

In this book you'll learn about both the creative and business aspects of screenwriting, including:

> The qualities a script MUST have to be seriously considered by a studio, television network or production company.

> How the process works once your script disappears into the Black Hole that is the film/television system.

> The fatal errors to avoid at all costs.

> How the film and television business really works.

> How to get your script read and seriously considered in Hollywood.

This candid look inside the movie and television business will answer those critical questions and many more. It is a vital aid for new writers, who will find it very user-friendly, and a source of new information and insight for the more experienced.

What you are about to learn in these pages can help to turn you from a novice into a professional screenwriter, and turn the story you're passionate about from a dream into a reality.

Pamela Wallace is a producer and the Academy Award-winning co-writer of Witness.

Acknowledgements

It seems that nearly everyone I meet knows someone who is writing a book or a script that deserves to be a theatrical or television movie. The public eagerly reads about the multimillion-dollar deals in Tinseltown and thousands of people pursue Hollywood's brass ring.

The truth with all such pursuits is that some will succeed and will, indeed, capture the dream of a career in film, television, or other media, but many others will not. Sometimes what is stopping a screenwriter is not his or her talent, but the lack of knowledge about the industry and how it works. I hope this second edition of *The Script-Selling Game* can help demystify and clarify the industry for you.

For four years I wrote a popular monthly column on The Biz, focusing mostly on screenwriting and development. I have had a chance to meet many readers of my columns at conferences and workshops, some of whom would show me the tattered copies of my columns they had put in a notebook or folder — all of them pleading with me to publish them in a book.

After much procrastination and prodding, and with a lot of encouragement and support, *The Script-Selling Game* was published in 2002. But as technology and invigorating interest in screenwriting has increased, so has the need for additional information to keep up with the times.

As is the case for most writers, I realized, with great clarity, just how fortunate I've been to have sustained a career in this roller coaster industry for more than thirty years.

I learned the true meaning of hard work and the importance of integrity from my former boss and mentor, Richard A. Shepherd, who gave me my first opportunity by opening a door and reminding me that it was up to me to do my best once I was inside.

I embraced the importance of sharing and giving from a very special "web" of industry consultants/friends: Dr. Linda Seger, Pamela Jaye Smith, Donie Nelson, Heather Hale, Todd Sharp, Scott Rice, Chris Vogler, Rachel Ballon, Ellen Sandler, Michael Ojakwe, Drew Yanno, Paula Berinstein, Marlowe Weisman, Debe Todd, Laurie Scheer, Michael Hauge, Madeline DiMaggio, Tony Chow, Terry Borst, and Carolyn Miller, while I have appreciated the enduring patience, understanding and friendship of my dear gal-pals, Pam Wallace, Gillian Arnold, Merrill Atlas, Juliane Bennett, Tamlyn Tomita, Leslie Kawai, Shirley Fong-Torres, Lori Crane, Beverly Bell, and my friends of the VGLDSW clan, who have kept me going even when I cursed this crazy business.

And the late Steve Lester and Meera Lester showed me the vision and dedication it takes to help others realize their dreams when they started their first-ever screenwriting conference, Selling To Hollywood, while Jesse Douma and the hard-working team at The Writers Store have always stepped up to the plate in showing their unwavering support not only for me, but for my colleagues and writers everywhere.

Through my workshops in more than a dozen countries around the world, I've come to realize how writers globally have the same overwhelming desire to unite and entertain us all through film, television and the media: Pierre Challain and Jean Michel Albert and the members of Thot Fiction; Signe Olynyk and her outstanding crew at The Great American Pitchfest; the producers, directors and writers of dozens of projects I've read through Europe's PILOT Programme; the hard-working writers and execs of RAI-TV Italy; the welcoming writers of Singapore, Thailand, Australia, Indonesia; and so many others who have given me a universal education and insight that has helped to shape my seminars as well as this new edition of my book.

And even before I knew that Hollywood would be my destiny, I have had the love and support of my Mom and Dad and the heartfelt treasure of tears and laughter from my sisters, Dana, 'trice, and Laureen.

To Michael Wiese, Ken Lee, Michele Chong, Debbie Beaver, Gina Mansfield, Matt Barber, John Brenner, and B. J. Markel — I cannot begin to thank you for continuing to believe in me and supporting my work. Your encouragement and respect means the world to me! And to Scott Baillie: Thanks for helping me to "make the connection," and to Jan Stiles, who edited my original columns: Thank you for your wise and magical "red pen." To my research assistant, Jason Wada: "You rock... and so does your band!" And to Robin Rindner: Thank you for the invaluable lessons to this tech-challenged writer on "merge," "page numbering," and "copying to disc."

Kathie Fong Yoneda
April 2011

Second Thoughts

I started having second thoughts about my book about a year after it was published in 2002. Animated films had just gotten the nod from the Academy for a separate category — Best Animated Feature Film. In addition to developing live-action films, I also worked extensively in developing animated projects while at Disney, and some of my workshops focused on animation.

In addition to teaching workshops on live-action and animation, I was also giving seminars that focused on television. I realized that while some of the basic information in *The Script-Selling Game* could be applied to both animation and television, there was so much more about those two subjects that my book needed to address.

Fast forward to a few years later: YouTube, MySpace and other Internet channels became an entertaining curiosity, and quickly became a part of our everyday life and culture.

So when MWP approached me about doing a second edition, I didn't have to think twice. I knew it was a golden opportunity to expand my book to include all of my "second thoughts," and to update and address some of the many questions and subjects that my writers have brought up in the last several years.

For those of you who have a 2002 copy of *The Script-Selling Game*, thank you for buying my book! And if you're asking yourself why you need to buy this second edition, here's a short list of reasons:

> A new chapter: "The Animation Revolution: So Much More Than Saturday Morning Cartoons" — an overview of the animation explosion; the difference between writing for animation and writing live-action; most popular animated genres; how to write springboards and premises, including examples, etc.

> Another new chapter: "Using the Internet: How The Web Can Be Your New B.F.F." — how to use the Internet to pitch your wares without leaving your home; opportunities for writing Web content, etc.

> A new section devoted to submitting your projects to television and cable.

> What's the difference between a spec/reading script and a shooting script?

> What's the difference between getting coverage and getting a consultation?

> More info on crafting a query letter, including an example.

> More examples on marketing tools like log lines, elevator pitches, and a new section on writing a selling synopsis.

> And yes, for those of you who enjoyed my opening chapter stories, I've included a few more of those as well!

To all of you writers who are holding this book in your hand, I hope you'll think of this as one of the wisest investments you can make — in yourself!

Chapter 1

Developing Ideas

One of my clients sent me her screenplay, a murder mystery, which was a real "page turner" and a major leap forward from her first two scripts. When I asked her for the genesis of this intriguing effort, she excitedly replied, "I found out my husband was having an affair, and I wanted to kill him, but my therapist told me to find another way to let out my feelings, so I killed him in my script!"

Who'd have thought of developing a great film idea through therapy?

The world has been making movies for well over a hundred years. And we now watch those movies not only in theatres, but also on television, cable, video, DVD, and even online. There are mail-order movie services where you can rent a movie, or you can simply take your iPad, laptop, iTouch or DVD player with you wherever you go. The worldwide audience desire for entertainment has never been higher. And behind all of this entertainment are ideas.

Moviemaking is big business, and before a studio is going to spend millions of dollars on a film, its executives want to hedge their bets. Hollywood has found that the best way to do that is to nurture a project from the very beginning. One Hollywood notable was quoted as saying that "In Hollywood, the idea is king." I would like to modify that statement slightly. In actuality, it is the *story* that is king.

Ideas are not even copyright-able, so it is hard to "own" or "claim" an idea. An idea is only a thought unless you build a viable story around it, populating it with characters who are caught up in a physical and/or emotional dilemma, giving them dialogue that says something funny, profound or meaningful, and most of all, providing the audience with a way to be moved and entertained.

Where do ideas come from?

Ideas for movies come from the same sources as all good story-telling — from experiences, both real and imagined. Starting with the cavemen boasting of their latest hunt or saving their families from a rock slide, right on up to blockbusters like the *Harry Potter* franchise, *Shrek*, *The Hangover*, *Avatar*, *Sherlock Holmes*, *The Blind Side*, *Iron Man*, *Casino Royale* and *Up*, good storytelling only differs in format. The cavemen used their rudimentary form of language and supplemented their "history" with drawings on the walls of their cave dwellings. Luckily, we have advanced, and can now use our computers to create novels and scripts.

Stories can emanate from past experiences, be fashioned around historical events, or placed in another era to show us the difficulties of a past or future time. A majority of the stories come from our present experience, from what is going on in our own world now. What successful film stories seem to share — no matter whether if they are set in the past, present or future — is the "human experience."

High concept/Low concept.

Writers are always asking me whether they should write a movie based on an idea that is "high concept" or "low concept." **High concept** usually means that the central story of the film can be easily summarized and will appeal to a larger audience. In other words, high concept movies are generally thought to be more commercial, and thus will bring in more moviegoers (and more money).

Low (or "Soft") concept is usually applied to a film that may focus on a more complex set of life circumstances or around a more specific issue — both of which can limit the numbers of people who might be interested in viewing the film.

However, as we all know, a more "commercial" movie is not always a "better" movie. Every February, the motion picture industry holds its collective breath as the nominations are announced for the Academy Awards. It should come as no surprise that most of the motion pictures nominated do not seem to fall into the big-budget "commercial" films that have grossed $200-million or more globally. Instead, most of the Best Picture nominations seem to favor those "smaller" specialty films, many of which were made for less than one-tenth the budget of their high-concept cousins.

In general, high concept can usually be defined as having a more "plot-driven" focus, while a low- or soft-concept project is usually more "character-driven." But there are exceptions to every rule and every generalization. Motion pictures like *The Blind Side*, *The Matrix*, *Titanic*, *Saving Private Ryan*, *Invictus* and *The Sixth Sense* succeeded because they found a successful balance and were both plot- and character-driven.

Adaptations.

Other sources for motion pictures are novels, myths, legends, the Bible, magazine articles, plays, songs, current events, and fairy tales. Whether a film is based on a *New York Times* best-selling novel or taken from a classic tale from Shakespeare, or surfaces as an updated version of a familiar legend or fairy tale, many screenwriters find inspiration in literature and stories of yore.

But adapting a project, especially based on written material that is not old enough to be in the public domain, can be somewhat tricky. If you want to adapt a best-selling novel into a screenplay, you will have to contact the publishing house to see if the film rights are available. If they are, you would be wise to contact an attorney who specializes in film rights to secure permission for you to adapt the novel. Surprisingly, some novelists (usually those whose books are not currently on the best-seller lists) have been known to allow a lucky screenwriter to option the rights to a script adaptation of their novel for as little as one dollar!

But anyone wishing to write a script based on already-published material should be warned: Studios will not touch a project if the writer has not secured the rights. The reason is obvious: A project without secured rights would be opening them up to a major lawsuit.

You should also tread carefully if you wish to base your project on a current event. While much of what we read in the newspapers or see on CNN can be considered public domain, you would be wise to check with an attorney, especially if you plan to focus on specific persons who are key figures in the event. While some people may not mind having a film based on their heroics or a tragic event in their life, others may find it an invasion of privacy.

If you have tried, without much success, to secure the rights to individuals connected to a current event, you may want to consider fictionalizing the story by creating your own characters, using a different perspective, and/or providing an unusual twist that would make your story more unique and possibly more dramatic.

What if...?

The best advice I can give to get a writer started on a new idea is to take the phrase, "What if...?" and fill in the rest of the sentence. The main reason most people enjoy going to the movies is that once we are in that darkened theater, we are hoping that we can be magically transported. Movies probe into our emotions, fears and imagination. And in the process, they sometimes serve as "wish fulfillment" (what if?) as we find ourselves sailing around the Caribbean on a ghost pirate ship with Johnny Depp in *Pirates of the Caribbean*, living in the dark underbelly of London as Robert Downey Jr. solves mysteries as *Sherlock Holmes*, defying the French culinary world with Meryl Streep in *Julie & Julia*, at the controls of *Apollo 13* with Tom Hanks, or in the Roman Coliseum fighting lions and demented emperors with Russell Crowe as a *Gladiator*.

Here are some examples of how some popular movies might have gotten their start if their creators had started out with the words "What if…?"

> What if… the teenage daughter of a U.S. President eludes her Secret Service detail in Europe in order to experience what "real life" is like on her own? (*Chasing Liberty*)

> What if… a ragtag group of unemployed Brits throws caution to the wind and decides to "bare it all" in order to earn some money as well as take back their self-respect? (*The Full Monty*)

> What if… an independent-thinking young rat sets out on his own with a dream of becoming a French chef? (*Ratatouille*)

> What if… a Roman soldier who loses his family finds a way to exact revenge on a cruel emperor by becoming a crowd-pleasing gladiator? (*Gladiator*)

> What if… a band of free-spirited deejays in the 1960s defies Great Britain's ban against rock music by illegally broadcasting from a boat just outside of the UK's boundaries? (*Pirate Radio*)

Many entertaining films (be they high or low/soft concept) are based on one of two situations:

> Taking an ordinary person and putting them in an extraordinary set of circumstances (e.g., *Twilight*, *Legally Blonde*, *Night at the Museum*, *Cast Away*, *The Last Samurai*).

> Taking an extraordinary person and putting them in an ordinary set of circumstances (e.g., *The Time-Traveler's Wife, E.T., Rain Man, Elf*).

What is "story"?

Once you have found an idea or several ideas to incorporate into your script, you will need a framework for your story. But what comprises a story? When I asked this question at a recent writers conference, most respondents quickly answered that story is "plot." While the plot is certainly one of the key aspects of a successful story, it is not the only element.

In general, a successful film story consists of the following:

> **Plot** — the situation, dilemma, or series of challenges in which the characters find themselves.

> **People** — whose job is to carry out the plot.

> Their **Surroundings** — their work, city/locale, family, etc.

> **Tone** — a balanced and somewhat consistent blend of responses and emotions to the plot.

While plot, people and surroundings are more evident in constructing a story, it is tone that often helps to elevate a story, providing the more recognizable emotional triggers that will entice and entertain an audience.

Themes/Emotions.

Many popular movies are based on themes that are connected to emotional situations and responses. From the beginning of the Greek and Roman myths to pop and hip-hop music, emotional responses have triggered creativity. Here are just a few examples of films that have benefited from strong, emotionally themed underpinnings:

> **Greed** — *Wall Street, There Will Be Blood, Double Indemnity*.

> **Revenge** — *Gladiator, Braveheart, Kill Bill.*

> **Sibling Rivalry** — *Brothers, In Her Shoes, Adaptation.*

> **Misfortune** — *Mad Max, The Full Monty, My Left Foot.*

> **Passion** — *Unfaithful, Body Heat, First Knight.*

> **Jealousy** — *Amadeus, Atonement, Ghost.*

> **Remorse** — *Unforgiven, Capote, Brokeback Mountain.*

There are dozens of other emotions or emotionally charged situations that can serve to drive your characters and plot, thus transforming your idea into a fully realized story. Referring to the tales that emanated from legends, folklore or mythology can serve as a touchstone to ignite your own film or television project.

The "Blockbuster" Movie.

I wish I had a penny for each time an emerging writer said, "Tell me how to write a blockbuster movie!" No one has a magic formula for writing a "blockbuster" movie, but there are some elements that most successful blockbusters seem to have in common:

> There must be broad audience appeal where the story can instantly "hook" a large portion of the moviegoing public and is not offensive or demeaning to a significant segment of the audience.

> The overall story offers something out of the ordinary, something you are unlikely to see on television. (Television movies are often on limited budgets and are not likely to include expensive action sequences, complex special effects, or sweeping cinematography.)

> Most blockbusters seem to be rooted in the following genres: action (the *Bourne* series), fantasy (*Avatar*), high-concept comedy (*Men in Black*) or a sweeping historical saga with tremendous "scope" (*Braveheart*). On occasion, a drama or romance can become a blockbuster (*Titanic* and *The Blind Side* are two such examples).

> Most blockbusters seem to be loosely structured with a mythical underpinning that the audience immediately recognizes and embraces (the *Star Wars* series and *The Godfather* trilogy are two obvious examples).

> The hero or heroine is someone the audience can easily relate to and empathize with (*Slumdog Millionaire*, *Forrest Gump*, *Precious*, *The Fugitive*). The inclusion of such overwhelming empathy for the protagonist is what is commonly called the "**root-ability factor**." Anti-heroes rarely make for blockbusters, although some may argue that *The English Patient* is one of those rare exceptions.

> The protagonists must be pitted against either a set of circumstances that are nearly overwhelming or against a villain who seems to have everything in his favor. A protagonist cannot be heroic if the challenges he faces (be they human or otherwise) are not truly worthy of that victorious happy ending.

> The tone of the movie (even if it is a comedy) should be smart, but not intellectual. There is a difference between a character who is *intelligent* and one who is *intellectual*. Audiences will get behind someone who may be intelligent but because of misfortune, finds himself at the bottom of the heap. They rarely will cheer on a character who displays only his intellect and not his vulnerabilities or "humanness."

> Most blockbusters usually have a satisfying ending. This does not necessarily mean a traditional happy ending, although happy endings are much more common. "Satisfying" can mean a bittersweet ending, wherein failure or tragic sacrifice is lightened by a sense of fulfillment. *Saving Private Ryan*, *Witness* and *Titanic* are three such examples of a bittersweet, but fulfilling, ending.

> And above all, a blockbuster should tap into and portray people's fears or fantasies, giving them a chance (at least for two hours) to live in a world or in a situation they have only imagined.

If you check out the highest grossing films of all time, more than half of the motion pictures listed will contain nearly all of the elements profiled above.

A reality check.

Although I have given you a list of elements that are common in blockbuster films, it is also important to realize that many of the movies on the "highest grossing" list were not initially thought to be blockbusters by their producers or studios.

Twentieth Century Fox was surprised and overwhelmed when respondents at the previews of *Star Wars* gave such high marks and positive comments to what Fox's marketing department thought would be "a nice family-style sci-fi movie." But when everyone from teenagers to baby boomers to grandparents gave the film some of the highest responses in history, Fox knew it had a potential hit on its hands. They quickly stepped up their marketing campaign and *Star Wars* has gone on to spawn one of the most successful franchises ever.

One of the most talked-about success tales involves the film *Forrest Gump*. Warner Bros. originally had the film on their development slate, but did not have much faith in the project and made the decision to put it in "**turnaround**" (put up for sale, usually to another studio that is willing to pay for any costs incurred up to that point). A rival studio, Paramount Pictures, quickly recognized the potential for the project and paid Warner Bros. its costs. Paramount went on to make the movie and was happy to add another Best Picture Oscar to its display case, as well as a huge grin at the movie's respectable standing among some of the highest grossing films of all time.

The Full Monty is another example of a film whose grosses stunned its distributors and producers. The heartfelt tale of a group of unemployed, small-town Brits who regain their self-respect and the love of the town's citizens by "baring all" was made for less than $3-million, but was eventually the most profitable film the year it was released. It is what the industry calls a "**sleeper**" — a slow-building, unexpected success.

Likewise, *My Big Fat Greek Wedding* was made for under $5-million and went on to gross more than $400-million worldwide. *Slumdog Millionaire* was made for $15-million and has grossed more than $380-million to date.

But what *Slumdog Millionaire*, *My Big Fat Greek Wedding*, *The Full Monty*, *Forrest Gump,* and *Star Wars* have in common (besides having grossed hundreds of millions of dollars at the box office) is that each of these projects has "heart." Their characters may have lived literally "light years" apart, but they all struggled with the need for respect and acceptance, and in their own way, gained the faith and courage to prove themselves.

There have been many writers whose motion pictures contained many of the elements that are common in blockbusters, yet their films did not succeed. On the other hand, there have been many movies that were initially considered "nice" or "small" or "quirky" which had something profound to say about the human condition, and, in turn, captured the audience's hearts and pocketbooks! So when considering an idea for a film project, be aware that there is plenty of room for both commercial and independent-type films. The moral of this chapter is: Whatever the story/idea, write it with passion and heart and not just thoughts of making money!

Chapter 2

Preparing For The Business Side Of Scripting

A young, emerging screenwriter had gotten "the call." As a result of his recent placing in a university short film competition, a vice president at a major studio (we'll call the exec Terry) had viewed the student film the screenwriter had written and directed and wanted to meet with him. The writer arrived for his meeting — late, nervous and unsure. When he arrived, the exec's door was open and the writer knocked and quickly entered the office where a man and a woman were waiting. The man, noting that the writer seemed flustered, asked if he would like something to drink. The writer turned to the woman and said he would like "coffee, black." A look was exchanged between the man and the woman, but the writer was too busy getting out his note cards to even notice. Trying to put the writer at ease, the woman told the writer how much they had enjoyed his film and asked if he had thought about expanding it into a full-length script. The writer said he had, and asked if he could pitch them his idea for the expansion into a movie. His pitch went well and he became more relaxed, but for most of the pitch, his body was angled mostly toward the man.

When it was time for the meeting to end, the writer gave a polite nod to the woman and said "Thanks" and then gave a handshake to the man and said, "Thanks so much, Terry. It was a pleasure to meet you." The man pointed to the female exec and said, "This is our vice president of production, Terry X... I'm Eric Z, director of development." The writer's face went red with embarrassment when he realized his mistake. Fortunately, they liked his student film and his pitch well enough that they said they would like to read his feature-length screenplay when it was completed. But this young writer learned a very valuable lesson: Do your research on who you'll be meeting with before you arrive!

In addition to writing a sure-to-be-a-hit screenplay, an emerging screenwriter would be wise to also prepare himself for what is known as "the business side of scripting." When faced with the prospect of sending out your "baby" to potential agents, entertainment attorneys, studios or production execs, do you know which people in which positions can help you the most? Do you know what kinds of budgetary limitations can play a role in whether your submission is a "Recommend" or a "Pass"? And are you aware of the role that the Writers Guild of America can play in your screenwriting career?

Knowing the answers to those questions can often put you and your projects one step ahead of the thousands of other eager scriptwriters who are also knocking eagerly on Hollywood's front gates.

Knowing the players.

The people in charge of making decisions on which projects will be bought are collectively called the "creative group." If you are targeting a production company, or if a studio exec is eager to hear about your newest project, you should definitely know who is part of this group and what its members do.

At the studios, the **creative group** consists of the head of the motion picture division, followed by the senior or executive vice presidents of production, the vice presidents of production, the directors of development (also referred to as creative execs) and the story editor. In a larger production company, you would have the producer (who is the principal owner), followed by either a senior vice president or vice president of production, a director of development and, occasionally, a story editor.

Where novice writers often make a mistake is targeting the "higher ups." In other words, they send their query letters or screenplays to the head of the motion picture division or the senior executives. If you have limited experience as a screenwriter, the better bet is to focus on the directors of development or story editors.

The senior executives will usually be dealing with the established writers, acting talent and producers. The directors of development and the story editors (who aspire to be senior executives or heads of studios or production companies) are more willing to search out and find new talent to prove themselves. In fact, discovering a new writer helps their own careers. It not only shows their bosses that they have uncommon initiative but also proves that they are willing to work harder to search out the talent that is necessary to "regenerate" the industry every few years. Eager to make a name for themselves, the execs on the lower rungs of the executive ladder are usually more eager ("hungrier") and tend to be risktakers.

Here's just a partial list of the creative group's responsibilities that directly affect a writer:

> Acquiring material that can be developed into motion pictures. The group reads scripts, treatments, plays, unpublished manuscripts, books, and news articles.

> Looking for new writing talent, mostly to fill any open writing assignments for an in-house idea or to rewrite or polish an existing project that requires a new writer. Besides reading scripts of new clients submitted by agents, the creative group also reads the scripts of the finalists from some of the major screenplay competitions, and "screens" (views) short films that are written and directed by film school students.

> Surfing the Internet to review new Web content that might have the potential to become a film or television project.

> Finding projects by taking pitch meetings with writers whose work they have read, hoping to get an early edge on a new project.

> Cultivating contacts at production companies, agencies and other studios to keep current on the latest acquisitions, newest acting/directing talent, and the constant changes in leadership.

Wooing the agencies and production companies.

Almost every emerging screenwriter (and especially those who live outside of the immediate Southern California or New York City areas) would love to send their material to an agent for possible representation. In discussing the art of doing business with agents, several screenwriters told me about their strategies for "wooing" the agencies and production companies.

If you have the time, patience and money, try calling some of the mid-level and smaller agencies. If you are unable to talk directly with an agent, you might try talking with his assistant. This may sound like a long shot, but many a successful writer has gotten a "break" from an assistant who was eager to prove himself as "agent material" to his boss by finding new talent on their own.

One playwright offered to give an agent two free tickets to his play which he had recently adapted into a script. When the assistant got on the line to tell the playwright that the agent had declined his offer, the playwright asked the assistant to be his guest. The result? The assistant not only enjoyed the play, but also asked to see the writer's screenplay adaptation and got his boss to read it. The agent ended up representing the playwright-cum-screenwriter. That assistant is now an agent at one of the larger agencies.

The same has also proven to work when it comes to assistants at production companies, since most assistants aspire to be development executives and producers. On a whim, an emerging screenwriter called the production company that had sent her a generic rejection letter. She asked to speak to the person who had signed the letter. It turned out to be the assistant to the producer. The writer asked him for some advice on the best way to get her material read and the assistant told her, "It's who you know." They chatted a little more about how hard it was to break into the business and the writer asked if the assistant would consider reading her script in exchange for a cup of coffee. The assistant took a chance. They met at a West Hollywood coffee café. Today the assistant is now a director of development at the same production company because he took a chance. He read a script, got his boss to read it, he optioned it, and recommended the writer to an agent friend who ended up representing her — all because she took some time to cultivate a relationship with the assistant.

However, wooing an assistant usually does not work if the assistant reports to someone at a higher-level agency or for the head of a production company or studio. Many of these assistants are what are known as "career" assistants who have no intention of becoming agents, producers or studio execs.

There is a saying in Tinseltown that one should never scoff at an assistant. You just never know when he will end up being your boss!

The business of making money.

While most writers feel that they should be generously rewarded for their submissions, the studios are obligated to make money for their stockholders. That responsibility means keeping an eagle's eye on production costs.

Did you know that the cost of the average studio theatrical motion picture without big name stars is close to $70-million? That is for a film set in present day, with a minimum of stuntwork and special effects, no animals, and probably no children in any major roles. With the ever-rising cost of making movies, it makes sense for the savvy writer to consider what constitutes a "high-ticket" project.

Although knowing how to budget does not fall within the technical realm of screenplay writing, the high cost of moviemaking is a subject that affects anyone connected with the motion picture and television industries.

Let's look at some general areas that can send a movie's budget soaring:

Period pieces/Futuristic settings.

This is an obvious high-ticket item in budgeting a theatrical or television/cable movie. A project set in the Middle Ages or Roaring '20s will require historically factual exterior and interior sets, props, modes of transportation, architecturally correct houses, and a time-specific wardrobe. Period pieces can also require additional research personnel.

While most major studios have sets for a Western town, a typical brownstone-lined New York avenue, or a Midwest main street, futuristic sets have to be assembled for each project. Stories set in the future carry the added cost of creating and making new props, backdrops, sets, furniture, vehicles, and costumes.

Exotic locations.

A spy thriller that takes place in five foreign cities also falls into the high-cost category. Although an audience loves to be swept away to an exotic land, the wise screenwriter sticks to one or two major locations. The exception, of course, is the "**road story**," in which characters are literally "on the road" from one location to the next as their story unfolds.

The role that time and budget constraints can play in challenging a writer is amazing. One popular film, *Three Days of the Condor*, was based on the book *Six Days of the Condor*, which involved several locations. In the interest of story clarity, timing and budget, writer Lorenzo Semple Jr. needed to make sure his script addressed these issues. He ended up selecting the three more important days/incidents in the book, which literally cut the story — and the budget — in half. The result was a highly entertaining and successful film that still maintained the book's original intent, suspense, and story integrity.

Children.

If your project has children in leading roles, you will need to remember that there are many strict guidelines and regulations that surround the filming of children. First, children are limited in the number of hours they are permitted to work per day. Thus, shooting with juveniles can take considerably more time. Overtime shooting is allowed only with a special permit and only if certain guidelines are met. And if there are night shots that require children, another permit is needed to accommodate night shooting.

The law also requires that an approved, paid tutor must be hired for all children on the set under the age of eighteen, unless they are "**emancipated minors**" (have a high school equivalency or have obtained court permission to be on their own). In addition to a tutor, a classroom must be set up, either at the studio or on location, and each child must receive a minimum of four hours of schooling per day. When minors are on the set, a child welfare supervisor must also be present.

Finally, we all need to remember that a child is a child. There can be a certain amount of unpredictability, depending on the child's age, disposition, and the shooting situation. For example, a young child told to run into a dark field on a chilly night may hesitate. The youngster may fear the dark, be too tired or cold, etc. Convincing a reluctant young actor who refuses to comply can be costly, especially if the writer ends up rewriting a scene.

But take heart — there are solutions. In some cases night scenes can be shot in daylight and merged with a night backdrop or shot with lighting that gives the appearance of night. A number of special "blue screen," "green screen," and "day for night" shots can be used to give the illusion of night, thus keeping the costs down.

Animals.

As with children, there are strict guidelines regarding the use of animals on the set — from a herd of stampeding horses to animal stars like "Fang," the mastiff who belongs to Hagrid in the *Harry Potter* movies, or "Marcel," the monkey who belongs to Ross on the sitcom *Friends*. A paid SPCA supervisor must be present during all shots requiring animals. Any scenes where an animal is depicted as "injured" or "dead" must be carefully choreographed and approved by the SPCA supervisor before any filming can take place.

Scenes involving animals can take much longer to shoot. In addition to the supervision of camera coverage, the SPCA worker also carefully notes any cruelty, misconduct or abuse in the handling, housing and transporting of animals. There are limitations on the types of stunts animals can do and the length of time they can work in front of a camera each day. It is interesting, too, that some animals have "doubles" for more specific tasks like limping, climbing, etc. Such was the case in the filming of the movie *Marly & Me*, where twenty-two yellow labs were used to portray Marly from puppy to full-grown dog and to perform a wide assortment of tasks and tricks.

Stuntwork.

Whenever there are fights, falls, chases, gunfights, fires or any dangerous action, stunt doubles are required to take the place of most actors and actresses. And while it appears that nearly every movie or TV show seems to contain at least one car chase or fist fight, the stuntwork in those scenes does drive up the cost of the project. A car chase or gun battle may take only a minute or two on the screen, but the actual time to set up, rehearse and shoot the sequence from different angles may take days.

Stuntwork is also highly dangerous, and stunt experts are well paid for their work. Unless you are intent on a big-budget action film, try to keep stuntwork at a minimum.

High-tech special effects.

We have all seen films where fifty people are gunned down in a hail of Uzi fire while gas tankers explode all around them and the hero makes a getaway on some high-tech, super-charged, futuristic vehicle at warp speed into another time dimension… and that is only the opening sequence! But not every action film is a guaranteed box office success. Satisfying what is viewed as the public's taste for mega-firepower no longer assures acceptance. High-tech effects alone will not sell your project, and the increased costs may actually do more harm than the effects do good.

The arena of high-tech special effects includes everything from fairly simple fade-outs to complex warp-speed chases in futuristic aircraft over the war fields of an unknown planet. Matte shots, blue/green screens, underwater sequences, explosions, disappearing or "morphing" objects, and any work requiring special cameras, models, miniatures or recreated objects constitutes the ever-growing area of high-tech and special effects.

Also, to ensure that projects are technically accurate and appropriate, advisors or consultants are often hired to give their expert advice and opinions on everything from the complex NASA control center in *Apollo 13* to the realistic dinosaurs in the *Jurassic Park* franchise to a specialist in ancient Mayan history for the film *2012*. For military dramas, armed services experts are often hired to maintain the integrity of the weaponry and personnel depicted on the screen.

The good news in this area is that computers have greatly cut the costs on some special effects, allowing for slightly greater latitude. With the advent and acceptance of growing technology, some special effects have become much more cost-effective than they were ten to fifteen years ago. Motion pictures like *300*, *Star Trek*, *Superman Returns*, *Casino Royale,* and *The Last Samurai* would have cost considerably more to produce if they were shot pre-2000.

But with the success of 3-D films such as *Clash of the Titans*, *How To Train Your Dragon*, *Avatar*, *Toy Story 3,* and *Alice in Wonderland*, the bad news is that ticket prices have increased and studios and distributors still have to make both traditional 2-D prints as well as the improved, but costlier, 3-D prints.

A cast of thousands.

Any project that requires hundreds of extras in crowd scenes carries an expensive price tag — think of having to provide wardrobe, props, makeup and hairdressers for those crowds. The average "extra" makes about $140 for a basic eight-hour day, not including the time needed for travel, additional wardrobe or makeup calls. If you multiple this by 250 extras, it would cost $35,000 just to shoot one crowd scene.

Any extra asked to do something "special" (which can be anything from a close-up reaction to "fainting" to being the leader in a mob scene) will receive considerably more compensation per day. Plus, all union extras receive benefits (such as health and pension) that are paid by the production company through the union, further driving up the price of those crowd scenes even more.

Balancing act.

The above list of big-ticket items is not meant to deter writers from creating memorable movies. They are meant as additional information in helping you to balance your plot and shape your project to make it even more desirable in the eyes of potential buyers. If your project contains more than three or four of these high-cost items, you may want to take a second look to see if there is any way to keep the expenses down.

What is the WGA?

Throughout this book you will see the initials "WGA." They stand for the Writers Guild of America. Members who live east of the Mississippi belong to WGA East (WGAe); members who live west of the Mississippi belong to WGA West (WGAw).

The WGA is the union representing writers primarily for the purpose of collective bargaining in the motion picture, television and radio industries. But the WGA has recently stepped in to represent writers of new media and animation as well.

New screenwriters who have yet to join the Guild often falsely assume that obtaining membership means instant and constant employment. While most major studios and larger production companies are signatories to the WGA and employ screenwriters who usually belong to the Guild, the number of writers far exceeds the number of assignments available. The WGA does not obtain writing assignments, offer writing instruction, nor accept material for submission to production companies.

Why is the WGA so important?

Once a screenwriter has obtained enough "units of credit" (currently 24 units within three years of application), he will likely join the WGA for the following reasons:

> WGA writers usually make considerably more than non-union members.

> WGA writers receive health and pension benefits. Non-union writers do not.

> WGA members can go through the Guild for any credit or payment disputes. Non-union writers will find it a costly venture for them when these kinds of disputes occur since they do not have the services of the Guild to intercede on their behalf.

> The WGA also helps its members to reacquire or buy back their work if their material is no longer in active development. If the material is for a theatrical film, this process is called a "reacquisition." If the material is for television or cable, this process is called a "reversion." Non-union writers would have little or no recourse to reacquire their work since they are not covered by the Guild.

How can the services of the WGA benefit a non-member?

Besides providing its members with basic minimum wage guidelines and working conditions, excellent benefits, and recognized authority in determining writing credits, the Guild also provides the following services (many of these services are made available to non-members as a courtesy for a small reasonable fee):

> The Television Market List features contact submission information on current weekly primetime television programs. This is published monthly in the WGAw magazine *Written By*, which non-members can also obtain for a nominal subscription fee. *Written By* also contains articles on industry issues, interviews with WGA members, and provides an FYI page listing helpful numbers for research.

> WGA Signatory Agency Listing features literary agencies that are affiliated with the WGA. This listing is updated several times a year and contains agencies that are currently open to submissions or queries from new writers. If you are not certain that an agent or agency you are dealing with is a WGA signatory, you can call the Guild and ask for the Agency Verification Department. If an "agent" asks for fees up front or violates any of the WGA guidelines, you can contact the WGA to file a complaint.

> The Professional Writer's Teleplay/Screenplay Format Guide features helpful information on the industry-accepted script format and is available to both members and non-members.

> The WGAw Registry is the world's leading script registration service. Since 1927, the WGAw has provided assistance to both members and non-members in establishing the completion date and the identity of their literary property. While this registration does not give a writer statutory protection, it does provide a record of a writer's claim to authorship of the material involved and of the date of its completion. Placing the words "Registered with the WGA" on the bottom corner of the title page of your script also is a subtle warning against possible plagiarism. Registration is currently $20 for non-members per project (outline, synopsis, teleplay, treatment, screenplay, etc.).

> In recent years, the WGAw Registry website has received a huge increase in usage. Screenplays and treatments from more than 100 countries around the world have been registered and the number of total submissions has increased to well over 70,000 pieces of new material per year.

> Minimum Basic Agreement provides the guidelines for employment, working conditions, and minimum basic wages for its members who work with signatory studios and production entities. Knowing what these minimum wages are can be especially useful if an emerging writer is lucky enough to have a producer or studio express interest in purchasing his work.

> Directory of WGA Members lists current WGA members and their produced credits. Producers and execs often use this directory when looking for a writer for an in-house idea or a polish or rewrite. This directory is also handy for writers who want to look up the writer of their favorite movie.

How can I obtain more information?

For more detailed information on the WGA and the services they offer, you can reach them at:

WGA WEST, 7000 West Third St., Los Angeles, CA 90048; (800) 548-4532; *wga.org*.

WGA EAST, 555 West 57th St. #1230, New York, NY 10019; (212) 767-7800; *wgaeast.org*.

Chapter 3

Pitching: A Necessary Evil

True story from a writer who wishes to remain anonymous: When he was getting started in the business and wanted to make an impression on a high-powered producer, the writer came in to "pitch" his baseball movie dressed in a baseball uniform, complete with ball and mitt. To start out his pitch he tossed the ball to the producer to get his attention and to emphasize that the name of the project was The Catch. Unfortunately, the writer's aim was off and the ball hit the producer's coffee mug, spilling java all over the place. The writer admitted he needed lessons in how to pitch — both literally and figuratively.

Pitching is the art of communicating (verbally or in writing) the essence of your screenplay or project, usually to an agent, studio executive or producer. While fewer projects are optioned on a pitch alone, more writers are pitching their wares as a means of enticing potential buyers to read their completed scripts.

Pitchfests — marathons of pitching to potential buyers — are also major components of many screenwriting conferences. **One-on-Ones**, ten-minute meetings with featured speakers or presenters, are also guaranteed "draws" for writers to attend and have the opportunity to tell Hollywood execs about their latest and greatest project.

Pitching, especially the verbal kind, does not come naturally to most writers. After all, writers seem to prefer to let their words-on-paper do most of the talking for them. With the high volume of scripts flooding the studios and major production companies every month, pitching has become "a necessary evil" for screenwriters to face and conquer.

Did you know that there are different types of pitches? And do you know when to utilize them to "sell" your work? Let's go over the types of pitching tools you are most likely to use.

Tool #1 — The "Log Line."

Your **log line** must tease the potential buyer, making him want to hear more of the story. In the following examples for the blockbuster *Avatar*, the quirky independent film *Away We Go*, and the whimsical animated movie *Finding Nemo*, notice how you can develop a log line by starting out with a short simple sentence.

Avatar — **Log line.**

Marine is given new assignment.

Paraplegic Marine is sent to a foreign moon on assignment.

Paraplegic Marine is dispatched to a foreign moon to infiltrate a colony of aliens.

Paraplegic Marine is dispatched to a foreign moon to infiltrate a colony of aliens who pose a threat to Earth.

Paraplegic Marine is dispatched to a foreign moon to infiltrate a colony of aliens who pose a threat to Earth, but eventually questions his mission.

Paraplegic Marine is dispatched to a foreign moon to infiltrate a colony of aliens who pose a threat to earth, only to question his mission when he realizes this peaceful new world poses no harm.

Away We Go — Log line.

Pregnant couple goes on road trip.

Pregnant couple, anxious about parenthood, goes on a road trip.

Pregnant couple, anxious about parenthood, takes a road trip, visiting various friends and relatives.

Pregnant couple, anxious about parenthood, takes a road trip, visiting various friends and relatives, hoping to ease their insecurities and find a place to settle down.

Hoping to ease their insecurities over the impending birth of their first child, a couple takes to the road, visiting friends and relatives in an effort to find their new home.

Hoping to ease their angst over the impending birth of their first child, a couple takes to the road, visiting an oddball assortment of friends and relatives — an odyssey which ends when they find the real meaning of family and home.

Finding Nemo — Log line.

Young fish is captured.

A father fish witnesses the capture of his young son.

When his young son is "fish-napped," a father clown fish sets out to rescue him.

Timid and cautious, a father clown fish sets forth on a danger-filled journey to rescue his impulsive son Nemo, who's been fish-napped and imprisoned in a dentist's aquarium thousands of miles away.

You will note that in each of the above examples, each successive sentence gains more importance and gives us a better understanding of the characters and a notion of the escalating storyline. The use of colorful, descriptive adjectives and verbs as well as creative restructuring of each sentence gives the log line more weight, flow, intensity, and interest.

Tool #2 — The "Elevator Pitch."

Similar to the log line is what is known as the **elevator pitch** — an expanded log line.

Imagine that you are attending a film festival. You get into the elevator of a posh hotel and notice there is only one other person in the elevator with you. It is the handsome Australian heartthrob, Sam Worthington, who just happens to be the perfect actor for the lead role in your very latest action project. He presses the tenth floor button. You recognize that this may be your golden opportunity. You have approximately fifteen to twenty seconds to tell him about your movie.

While this scenario may seem highly unlikely, having less than a minute to tell someone about your project is a very common situation. Would you be able to tell your story in less than a minute? For many writers, this is sheer terror. But, with preparation, the "elevator pitch" can be one of your most useful selling tools. Here is an "elevator pitch" which might have enticed Sam Worthington into taking the lead role in *Avatar*.

EXAMPLE: Assigned to infiltrate a potentially dangerous colony of aliens on a foreign moon, a paraplegic Marine is torn between obeying his orders and protecting the spiritual tribe with whom he has bonded. His friendship with a female alien deepens into love, and in a final showdown, he risks all to help the aliens save their homeland.

An elevator pitch should not take more than fifteen to twenty seconds to pitch and should be no more than a few sentences in length. You will notice that the first sentence clearly lays out the major storyline and even brings in the main character's motivating backstory which will propel him throughout most of the movie. The second sentence also provides the groundwork for the subplot: the romance between Sam Worthington's character and the female alien. The overall pitch signals an intriguing plot that combines danger, action, suspense, and romance featuring a deeply torn lead character who must risk his life by changing his long-held loyalties.

The elevator pitch is what many writers use at the fast-paced pitchfests where the producers and development execs only want to hear a couple of sentences about your project before deciding if they want to hear more details. The elevator pitch is a slightly longer log line that can serve as a setup for your three-minute pitch.

A written version of the elevator pitch can also be used as a major component of a writer's query letter to producers or agents, which brings us to the next tool in a your arsenal.

Tool #3 — The "Pitch On Paper."

Many a well-prepared writer has given thanks to those fickle screenwriting muses for having a **P.O.P.**, or "pitch on paper." A pitch on paper is a brief, one-page synopsis of your project which has just enough details to whet a producer's or agent's appetite and to distinguish your project from others.

Basically the P.O.P. consists of the following:

> A log line that gives the potential buyer a general idea of the storyline.

> The first paragraph contains the setup of the story — the main character, his present situation, his enemy/foe, where the story takes place, and the characters and incidents that move the main character into action.

> The second paragraph is an overview of the various challenges the hero or heroine must face in the midsection of the movie.

> The third paragraph is a quick summation of the ending or a summation of Act Three that ends with an intriguing question or situation designed to leave the climax to the imagination of the potential buyer.

Here are examples of a P.O.P. from two successful films — the classic romantic comedy *Sleepless In Seattle* and the blockbuster, futuristic action-adventure flick *Avatar*.

Sleepless In Seattle — Pitch On Paper

LOG LINE: A young boy's call to a radio psychologist sets into motion a series of events which could unite his widowed father with a magazine writer. Only a couple of things stand in the way: The boy and his father live in Seattle and the writer is already engaged and lives in Baltimore.

SAM is a Seattle architect, a widower, and father to young JONAH. Jonah recognizes that his father is lonely. Troubled, Jonah calls one of those late-night radio psychologists and talks about how worried he is for his dad. In Baltimore, magazine writer ANNIE and her FIANCÉ have just announced their engagement to her family. As she is driving home, she tunes into the talk show and feels a connection to Sam. Annie's best friend BECKY suggests that she do an article on radio talk shows. Realizing that Jonah is right and he needs to get on with his life, Sam contemplates dating again.

Sam takes the plunge and calls the DECORATOR on one of his projects. She ends up asking him for a date. Annie writes a letter to "Sleepless in Seattle," the radio psychologist's nickname for Sam, but tosses it in the trash. Becky rescues the letter and sends it off to Seattle. Unable to get "Sleepless in Seattle" out of her mind, Annie arrives in Seattle to do her story. She sees Sam embracing another woman and quickly returns home.

Annie plunges back into her wedding planning with her Fiancé, while Sam makes plans to spend the weekend with the Decorator, much to the disappointment of Jonah, who sneaks out of the house and takes a flight to NYC, hoping to meet Annie at the top of the Empire State Building. Will Sam realize where Jonah has gone? Will Annie listen to her heart? And will Sam and Annie finally meet?

Avatar — Pitch On Paper

LOG LINE: Assigned to infiltrate a potentially dangerous colony of aliens on a foreign moon, a paraplegic ex-Marine questions his mission when he is torn between obeying his orders and protecting the colony, which he has come to regard as his new home.

Paraplegic ex-Marine JAKE SULLY takes his late twin brother's place in a scientific project on a foreign moon. Jake will be part of an important program where he will become a genetically-bred Avatar so he will look like a Na'vi alien. The program is run by DR. GRACE AUGUSTINE, who also has an Avatar body. Jake meets corporate security head COLONEL QUARITCH, who claims the Na'vi are dangerous and must be killed. He tells Jake that if he uses his presence among the Na'vi to get him information on their culture, he will make sure Jake will get the surgery he needs to walk again. Jake agrees to do so. Awkward at first, Jake gets used to his Avatar body. He strays from Grace and reacts violently when confronted by a pack of Viperwolves. Na'vi princess NEYTIRI saves him, but chides him for being a baby and for killing unnecessarily. But she senses he has a strong heart and has no fear. Her assessment is validated when the sacred seeds of Eywa gravitate to Jake. She takes him to Hometree, the Na'vi's main habitat, and he is accepted when Neytiri's mother MO'AT declares that Jake can live with them, and that Neytiri will be responsible for teaching him their language and customs. Neytiri accepts this responsibility with reluctance.

Meanwhile, corporate rep PARKER SELFRIDGE is under the gun to start mining for a valuable mineral, Unobtanium, the largest source of which is located under Hometree. He thinks the Avatar team is moving too slowly in getting the Na'vi to move to a different location. Grace moves the Avatar team to the floating mountains, closer to the Na'vi. Jake learns the language quickly and comes to understand the Na'vi's connection to the plants and animals. Neytiri declares he is ready to connect with a Banshee, a flying creature. It is a dangerous rite of passage, but he succeeds. While riding his Banshee, he learns to avoid TORUK, an even larger flying creature. Neytiri says her grandfather rode Toruk to unite the five Na'vi tribes many years ago. Neytiri is proud of Jake's progress, but Quaritch now has the information he needs to destroy Hometree. At the sacred Tree of Souls, Jake and Neytiri finally mate and accept their love. The next morning, bulldozers come to destroy the area at the Tree of Souls. Jake stops the bulldozers, but Quaritch recognizes Jake. Jake returns to the lab and begs Parker to let him persuade the Na'vi to move away. He is given an hour. Unfortunately, Jake and Grace are bound to a stake by the Na'vi. Quaritch and his flying platoon destroy Hometree. Mo'at releases Jake and Grace and begs them to save the Na'vi. Neytiri's father is killed. Back at base, Jake and Grace are arrested.

Pilot TRUDY CHACÓN, who did not sign on to kill innocent aliens, frees Jake and Grace and flies them to the Na'vi. They are met with skepticism, but Jake asks them to save Grace, who was wounded in the escape. They take her to the Tree of Souls, but it is too late and she dies. Jake successfully bonds with the Toruk and returns to the Na'vi. But is he too late to help the Na'vi rally the other tribes? And how can the Na'vi possibly win against Quaritch and his massive high-tech weaponry?

In both examples, you will notice that most of the storyline is set up in the first paragraph and fewer details are given in the second and third paragraphs. Each of the paragraphs coincides with the basic three-act structure: beginning, middle, and end.

Some writers prefer to do one long paragraph for their pitch on paper, which is basically three to five sentences on each act. A P.O.P. is sometimes given to a potential buyer at the end of a pitch meeting to help the producer or exec refresh his or her memory after a day of hearing several pitches. Some agents or smaller production companies might be intrigued by your query letter, but are not yet willing to take the time to commit to looking at a 110-page script, in which case they may ask you for a one-page summary (P.O.P.) of your project.

Tool #4 — The "Synopsis."

There will be times when you will need more than a one-pager, but less than a treatment of your project. This document is called a **synopsis**.

What is a "synopsis"?

A synopsis is very much like those book reports we used to do in high school. It is a summation of the major highlights of the story, told in a positive, hopefully engaging manner that will convince someone to read your treatment or screenplay.

Why is it important to have a synopsis of my project?

While attending a number of recent writing conferences, pitchfests and screenwriting events, I have noticed that book editors, agents and production execs on the prowl for hot new material are limited by the amount of time it takes to read a full-length screenplay or a several hundred page manuscript. In some instances, they have requested a synopsis, stating that a two- to three-page synopsis would be a more helpful document for them to consider than a P.O.P.

In addition to the fact that a synopsis is a timesaver, execs found that reading a synopsis could also give them a better idea of a writer's "style." As one agent confided, it was her experience that some writers could come up with a great log line, but many times she would be disappointed when she read the actual screenplay or manuscript. Having a synopsis not only helped to flesh out the storyline, but gave her a much better idea of the writer's storytelling style and his ability to develop characters and advance the plot.

While a one-pager is a good way to know the basic plot of the writer's material, a two- or three-page synopsis is an even better indication of more specific elements that could possibly set this project apart from others of the same genre.

But isn't a synopsis the same as a treatment?

A synopsis is generally no more than two to three pages in length, whereas most treatments are at least five to ten pages or more in length. A synopsis has more details of the plot than a P.O.P., but treatments will be even more detailed and sometimes will include a line or two of dialogue to give "color" and "flavor" and a sense of drama/comedy, or attitude that will typically run through the entire project. Treatments will spell out every major plotline and every sub-plotline and will include nearly all characters with speaking parts.

What are the key elements of a selling synopsis?

▸ Like a P.O.P., a synopsis usually starts off with a log line or elevator pitch.

▸ The first paragraph should give an indication of the time period, unless the story is set in present day, which needs no such indication.

▸ The first paragraph or two should include the area(s) where a majority of the action takes place.

- ▸ All major characters should be introduced in the first few paragraphs.

- ▸ The main character's goal should be clearly apparent by the end of Act One.

- ▸ The "B" storyline is usually set up by the end of Act One, or, at the latest, in the first half of Act Two.

- ▸ The midsection of your synopsis is where you will spend about three to four paragraphs setting up the escalating obstacles and challenges that your character(s) will face in Act Two.

- ▸ At the end of Act Two, your synopsis should indicate the ultimate challenge being faced by the protagonist.

- ▸ The last couple of paragraphs of your synopsis should cover the denouement of your story and wrap up any loose ends of your major plotline and any subplots.

- ▸ It is up to you if you would like to "tease" the potential buyer by ending the synopsis with an intriguing question or two that "lead" the reader to the appropriate ending. Some writers prefer to use a conventional approach that gives us a clearer sense of how the story ends.

- ▸ Please note that certain genres help to define the length of a synopsis. Shorter synopses are used for romantic comedies, love stories and family-friendly films, while mysteries, thrillers, action-adventure, historical pieces and sci-fi/fantasy projects tend to increase the length of a synopsis.

How can a synopsis be used?

If you are attend a writing conference or pitchfest, an agent or producer may ask for a synopsis (or occasionally, a treatment) of your project if they liked your log line, elevator pitch or verbal pitch.

But probably the most important use of a synopsis is to register your project with the Writers Guild of America to establish a timeline for your creative efforts. Most professional writers will immediately register a synopsis of their latest project, even if they have not yet completed the entire screenplay. Once they have finished their script, they will register the screenplay. Registering your material comes in handy, should that rare situation arise when you feel your project has been compromised or stolen.

Word to the wise: Do not submit a synopsis of your project unless it is requested. If an agent or potential buyer requests a full-length screenplay, do not submit a synopsis to accompany the script. Unfortunately, if a buyer happens to spot both a synopsis and the full material of the same project, and if she is under a time crunch, she may be tempted to read only the synopsis and may very well leave your actual script unread.

Using the previous P.O.P. examples of *Sleepless In Seattle* and *Avatar*, here is how you can expand your pitch on paper into a synopsis (PLEASE NOTE: Most of the text is from the original P.O.P. examples; sections in **bold** are the additions to the one-pager):

Sleepless in Seattle — **Synopsis.**

LOG LINE: In this romantic comedy, a young boy's call to a radio psychologist sets into motion a series of events which could unite his widowed father with a journalist. Only a couple of things stand in the way — the boy and his father live in Seattle and the writer is already engaged and lives in Baltimore.

SAM, **early 30s,** *is a Seattle architect, a widower, and loving father to young JONAH.* **As the Christmas season draws near,** *Jonah recognizes that his father is lonely. Troubled, Jonah calls one of those late-night radio psychologists,* **DR. MARSHA,** *and talks about how worried he is for his dad.* **Dr. Marsha asks Jonah to put Sam on the phone. Reluctant to open up, Sam eventually is coaxed into talking about his late wife and we realize he is still grieving, even though it has been almost two years since his wife died.**

In Baltimore, journalist ANNIE (late 20s) and her fiancé WALTER **(as nice as they come and allergic to nearly everything)** *have just announced their engagement to her loving but eccentric family.* **Annie's MOTHER takes her to the attic where Annie tries on her Granny's vintage wedding dress. Annie's Mom talks about her own romance with Annie's FATHER and mentions the "magic" between them from the start, but Annie doesn't seem to be experiencing that same "magic" as she contemplates** *her future with Walter. As Annie is about to take off the wedding dress, it tears and she can't help but wonder if this is a "sign" of some sort.*

As she's driving home, she tunes into the talk show and feels a connection to Sam, **who mentions the "magic" he felt with his late wife.** *Following the* **holidays, Annie attends an assignment meeting, chaired by her best friend and coworker BECKY, who talks about how the phone lines in Chicago were tied up over Dr. Marsha's call with "Sleepless in Seattle." Annie admits that she couldn't stop listening to the show and Becky** *suggests that she do an article on radio talk shows,* **much to the chagrin of her male co-workers WYATT and KEITH, who make jokes about how desperate women are these days.**

Realizing that Jonah is right and he needs to get on with his life, Sam contemplates dating again. **He has a man-to-man talk with good friend JAY, who warns him that dating is very different now. Meanwhile, Annie talks to her brother DENNIS about her pre-wedding jitters and she talks herself into thinking her worries are unfounded.**

Sam takes the plunge and calls **VICTORIA,** *a decorator on one of his projects. She* **eagerly** *ends up asking him for a date.* **Annie does research on the computer and learns that Sam's last name is Baldwin. She hires a detective to learn more about him. Although the detective sends her a blurred photo of Sam having dinner with Victoria (we can only see the back of her head),** *Annie* **can't quite get Sam out of her mind and she** *writes a letter to "Sleepless in Seattle," but tosses it in the trash* **while she and Becky are watching the romantic melodrama An Affair to Remember.** *Becky rescues the letter and sends it off to Seattle,* **where it arrives with dozens of sacks of letters, all addressed to "Sleepless in Seattle." Jonah and his friend JESSICA love Annie's letter, which mentions meeting at the top of the Empire State Building on Valentine's Day. Without consulting Sam, they send a reply to Annie.**

Becky calls Annie in the middle of the night to let her know that Jonah has called Dr. Marsha again. Annie listens and realizes that she is *unable to get "Sleepless in Seattle" out of her mind. Annie arrives in Seattle to do her story. Sam, who has just seen Victoria off at the airport, spots Annie and is attracted to her, but loses her in the crowd.* **Later, Annie** *sees Sam embracing* *another woman (**actually his sister**) and she quickly returns home, thinking all is lost.*

*Annie plunges back into her wedding plans with **Walter, meeting him in NYC during Valentine's weekend to select their wedding china at Tiffany's**. It becomes apparent to Annie that although Walter is one of the nicest men around, their future would be too predictable and there does not seem to be any "magic" in their relationship. She has a heart-to-heart talk with Walter, who assures her that he does not want to marry her if she is only "settling" for him. She decides to throw caution to the wind and takes a taxi to the Empire State Building.*

*Meanwhile, Sam is packing to spend the weekend with **Victoria**, much to the disappointment of Jonah, who sneaks out of the house and, **with Jessica's help,** takes a flight to NYC, hoping to meet Annie at the top of the Empire State Building. **As Sam is instructing the Babysitter, he realizes that Jonah is missing.** Will Sam realize where Jonah has gone? Will Annie listen to her heart? And will Sam and Annie finally meet?*

Avatar — Synopsis.

LOG LINE: Assigned to infiltrate a potentially dangerous colony of aliens on a foreign moon, a paraplegic ex-Marine questions his mission when he is torn between obeying his orders and protecting the colony, which he has come to regard as his new home.

*After a combat spinal injury, paraplegic ex-Marine **JAKE SULLY finds himself in a "Catch-22" situation — he cannot work because of his injury, and he is unable to afford the surgery to repair his spinal cord so he can find a job. Then he is offered an opportunity to take** his late twin brother's place on a scientific project on a foreign moon. **Jake's DNA is the same as his brother's, which means he can become** part of an important program where he will become a genetically-bred Avatar so he will look like a Na'vi alien. **The Na'vi are ten feet tall, with blue skin, and a long thin tail. They are extremely agile.** The program is run by DR. GRACE AUGUSTINE, who also has an Avatar body, **as does program teammate NORM SPELLMAN. To become an Avatar, Jake, Grace and Norm must lie in a pod where their brain waves are connected to the Avatar bodies which are specially equipped*** *to adapt to the breathing needs on Pandora. Grace, Norm and Jake are to learn the language and as much as they can about the Na'vi, their culture, beliefs, and the unique world in which they live on Pandora. Jake is also required to do daily video updates on his experiences with the Na'vi people and their sacred region.*

Jake meets **staunch, inflexible** *corporate security head* COLONEL QUAR-ITCH, *who claims that the Na'vi are dangerous and must be killed.* **Appealing to Jake's military background,** *he tells Jake that if he uses his presence among the Na'vi to get him information on the aliens, he will make sure Jake will get the surgery he needs to walk again. Jake agrees to do so. Awkward at first, Jake gets used to his Avatar body.* **Jake meets TRUDY CHACÓN, a retired pilot, who drops off the Avatar team on Pandora. While on assignment, Jake** *strays from Grace and reacts violently when confronted by a pack of Viperwolves.* **Things become more dangerous when a larger creature pursues him and he has to jump from the top of a waterfall to escape.** *Na'vi princess* NEYTIRI, **who has been tracking Jake,** *saves him, but chides him for being a baby and for killing unnecessarily. But she senses he has a strong heart and has no fear. Her assessment is validated when the sacred seeds of Eywa gravitate to Jake. She takes him to Hometree, the Na'vi's main habitat, and he is* **welcomed by EYTUKAN, Neytiri's father, and** *accepted when Neytiri's mother* MO'AT *declares that Jake can live with them, and that Neytiri will be responsible for teaching him their language and customs. Neytiri accepts this responsibility with reluctance.* **As night falls, Trudy, Grace and Norm must abandon their search for Jake until the next morning — if he is lucky enough to survive the night.**

Meanwhile corporate rep PARKER SELFRIDGE *is under the gun to start mining for a valuable mineral, Unobtanium. The largest source is located under Hometree. He thinks the Avatar team is moving too slowly in getting the Na'vi to move to a different location.* **Angry that Parker and Quaritch are unable to understand the importance of the Avatar program,** *Grace moves the Avatar team* **and its lab** *to the floating mountains, closer to the Na'vi.* **With Neytiri's help,** *Jake learns the language quickly and comes to understand* **and respect** *the Na'vi's* **spiritual** *connection to the plants and animals. Neytiri declares he is ready to connect with a Banshee,* **a large green** *flying creature* **which each**

Na'vi warrior has. *It is a dangerous rite of passage, but he succeeds* **and gains the begrudging respect of the other Na'vi warriors, including TSU'TEY, who would likely succeed as leader of the Na'vi in the event of Eytukan's death. Tsu'Tey has also made it known that he is attracted to Neytiri.** *While riding his Banshee,* **Jake** *learns to avoid TORUK, an even larger* **magnificent red** *flying creature. Neytiri says her grandfather rode Toruk to unite the five Na'vi tribes many years ago.*

Neytiri is proud of Jake's progress **and it is evident that there is an attraction between them. Jake has come to love and respect the Na'vi and their peaceful way of life, realizing that they are not the violent aliens which Quaritch wants to decimate. However, Jake's change of heart comes too late as** *Quaritch now has the information he needs to destroy Hometree,* **thanks to Jake's video logs.** *At the sacred Tree of Souls, Jake and Neytiri finally mate and accept their love. The next morning, bulldozers come to destroy the area at the Tree of Souls. Jake stops the bulldozers, but Quaritch recognizes Jake. Jake returns to the lab and begs Parker to let him persuade the Na'vi to move away. He is given an hour. Unfortunately,* **none of the aliens believe Jake and Grace and they** *are bound to a stake by the Na'vi. Quaritch and his flying platoon destroy Hometree.* **As she flees Hometree,** *Mo'at releases Jake and Grace and begs them to save the Na'vi. Neytiri's father is killed. Back at base, Jake and Grace are arrested* **and thrown in confinement.**

Pilot Trudy, who did not sign on to kill innocent aliens, frees Jake, **Norm** *and Grace and flies them to the Na'vi. They are met with skepticism* **by the Na'vi,** *but Jake asks them to save Grace who was wounded in the escape. They take her to the Tree of Souls* **in an attempt to transfer her human soul into her Na'vi body to save her,** *but it is too late and she dies.* **Determined to keep his vow to Mo'at to save the Na'vi, Jake uses his Banshee and, in a daring maneuver, he** *successfully* **captures and** *bonds with the Toruk and returns to the Na'vi.* **He pleads with Tsu'Tey, Neytiri, Mo'at and the rest of the Na'vi to help him. He will unite the other tribes. Because he knows the kind of weapons and equipment used by "the sky people" (the human security forces led by Quaritch), he will help the Na'vi, even if he has to die with them. Before the battle begins, Jake goes to the Tree of Souls and prays to Eywa that the Na'vi will survive.**

As Quaritch and his forces fly into battle, Jake and the Na'vi warriors on their flying creatures attack from above. The battle becomes heated and Neytiri is thrown from her beloved banshee. Trudy swoops in and opens fire, wreaking havoc. But eventually her ship is hit and she plummets to her death. Jake finds Neytiri on the forest floor. Quaritch's troops on the ground are coming closer, but are suddenly overwhelmed by stampeding herds of Pandora's animals. Jake successfully launches a few well-placed grenades which down the bombship before it can get to the Tree of Souls, but Quaritch escapes in his mega exo-skeletal shell. He and Jake do battle and the shell is rendered useless. Quaritch dons a breathing apparatus and heads for the Avatar lab to try and detach human Jake from his Avatar. Neytiri uses her poisoned arrows and kills Quaritch before he can kill Jake. She gives Jake a breathing device to save him.

With the corporate military base under Na'vi leadership, the remaining humans are returned to earth, while several of the more sympathetic and enlightened humans decide to stay on Pandora. In his final video log, Jake voices his decision to permanently become a Na'vi. The aliens surround him at the Tree of Souls as he successfully passes through the "eye of Eywa" and awakens in his Avatar form, to become their leader, with Neytiri by his side.

Tool #5 — The "Big Pitch."

For those situations when you have a one-on-one consultation or you are meeting with a potential buyer who is intrigued by your log line or elevator pitch and wants to hear more, you should be ready for the "**Big Pitch**."

Writers should approach the Big Pitch as a "verbal trailer" for the film they envision. Like the visual "trailer" of "coming attractions," the Big Pitch should contain the highlights of the story you are telling and it should be told with confidence and style.

Going to websites like *moviefone.com* or *imdb.com* can be of huge assistance. Once you are at one of the two websites, do a "search" for a successful movie in the same genre as your project. Then click on the link to the movie's "trailer" and watch it. You will notice that most trailers last roughly two or three minutes (coincidentally, about the same amount of time as a pitch) and usually contain anywhere from five to eight "highlights" of the storyline. This should give you a general idea of the plot points or character revelations that you might want to extract from your very own script for your pitch.

Some writers will compose a one-page outline of their pitch, using brief phrases to describe the highlights they wish to use in pitching their storyline. Other writers use a similar technique, but divide up their outline into Act One, Act Two, and Act Three, making it easier to refer to the outline, should they become momentarily lost during the presentation of the pitch.

It goes without saying that a concise, well-told story can either open or close those career doors for a writer. Here are some pitching pointers if you are fortunate enough to be invited to pitch your project at a studio or production company:

Be concise.

Know in advance that most pitch meetings will last less than a total of twenty to thirty minutes tops. Most of the meeting will consist of general introductory small talk before the pitch. In most cases, the actual pitch will take anywhere from five to seven minutes. In a pitch-fest where there is a shorter time frame, you will need to keep your pitch closer to the three-minute mark. After the pitch, time is allowed for any questions or suggestions from the potential buyer, followed by some parting comments or questions from you, the writer.

Know your audience.

Research the studio or production company where you will be pitching. What kinds of movies or television projects do they produce? More importantly, what kinds of projects do they *not* produce?

For example, a writer once made the mistake of pitching a slasher movie to the execs at Walt Disney Pictures. Needless to say, it was an immediate "Pass" and left the executives with the impression that the writer had not spent much time researching the studio's development slate.

There is no excuse for not researching a studio or production company in advance of a meeting. *The Hollywood Creative Directory* lists credits for produced work beneath each production entity's name. And many production companies now have websites listing their produced credits. The key is to look for studios and production companies who have shown an interest in producing films/projects in the same genre as your own.

In addition, it is important to keep up to date on any "deals" that a studio or production company may have made recently, especially with actors or directors who may have a production company on the premises. Reading the trade papers (*The Hollywood Reporter*, *Variety*) can often yield this type of valuable information. Again, *The Hollywood Creative Directory* has a section in the back that cross-references personnel with the names of production companies and studios with whom they are connected.

Practice makes perfect.

It is common sense: Practice your pitch beforehand. It is best to practice in front of people who are *not* familiar with your story. This rehearsal will help to focus on any sticky plot points or confusing storylines.

While practicing in front of your parents, spouse or siblings can provide some comfort and reassurance, you will get a much more honest appraisal of your work if you pitch your project in front of your writers group or a friend who works in marketing or sales.

Be sure to ask the following questions after practicing your pitch in front of anyone:

> Did they have any comments or suggestions?

> Did they get a feel for the characters?

> Did they understand what the hero/heroine was trying to accomplish?

> Did any sections of the pitch feel too slow or too fast?

> Was the storyline logical and clearly laid out, or were there any confusing pieces of plotting?

> Is this a movie that they would pay to see?

> If not, why not?

Have a backup.

Be ready to pitch two projects, knowing that you will probably only have time to pitch one. This preparation is especially handy when you have invested time and money in attending a pitchfest.

Why have a backup pitch? If the executive or agent you are pitching to does not appear attentive when you are halfway through, you can quickly wind up your story and go on to your next project.

Also, you never know when a potential buyer will ask if you have other projects in the works. A true writer always has several projects in the works.

Show some style.

Be enthusiastic when you pitch. Keep in mind that studio and production execs listen to as many as five to six pitches every day. Having heard thousands of pitches, I can assure you that there is nothing worse than someone who is mumbling his story into his lap.

You can ham it up a bit, but do not let your theatrics over-shadow your story. Here's an instance of someone who went "over the top":

The project was a modern-day version of the popular fairy tale *Cinderella*. Every time the Fairy Godmother was mentioned in the pitch, the writer threw "magic dust" into the air and waved a "magic wand." By the end of the pitch, my hair and my office were covered with gold and silver glitter. I remembered the pitch — but obviously, not for the right reasons.

Here's a case of someone who used just the right amount of theatrics:

To emphasize her nostalgic 1960s setting, a writer started out by playing the first sixteen bars of a popular song from that era before launching into her pitch. She's not sure if the musical introduction was responsible, but it got the executive to listen attentively to her pitch... which was optioned on the spot!

Remember to speak clearly — not too quickly and not too slowly. Look at the buyer when you are pitching. It is fine to refer to your notes or your pitch on paper or pitch outline from time to time, but do not "read" your movie to us.

Start with a log line.

Start off with your log line, which should accurately convey the essence of your movie as well as a sense of why the public should rush to see your project. Think of the "one-sheets" (giant posters) that advertise the movies.

Some writers often use other successful projects to convey a sense of story and tone. I don't know if this rumor is true or not, but I was told the execs at ABC Network loved the following log line for a TV series, which utilized two well-known produced properties:

EXAMPLE: In this dramedy series, *The Stepford Wives* give the gals from *Sex and the City* a run for their money! (*Desperate Housewives*)

Go on to the basics.

Next, state the genre, time period, and where a majority of the action takes place.

EXAMPLE: This contemporary, bicoastal romantic comedy takes place in Seattle and Baltimore. (*Sleepless in Seattle*)

It is important to state the genre at the beginning of the pitch as a means of setting the scene and the tone of the project. I once had a meeting with a writer who obviously hated pitching and did not show much inflection or emotion in his pitch. Thus, I thought the project was a drama and informed him that we had recently bought a number of dramatic projects. We both were embarrassed when he declared that his project was, in fact, a comedy!

Introduce your main characters.

Introduce your main characters with a brief but "telling" description that gives us the following information: age range, major personality traits, job/career, etc.

EXAMPLE: Harry Potter, 11, is anxious, but eager, to leave the confines of his room under the stairs at his Aunt's and Uncle's house to discover his destiny at Hogwarts School of Witchcraft and Wizardry (*Harry Potter and the Sorcerer's Stone*).

And while there is no need to introduce every single character in your screenplay, do not forget to include the antagonist and any secondary characters who have a major impact on the storyline.

Hit the high notes.

Stick to the major plot points and character revelations only. There is no need to describe each and every scene, but any subplot that is key to the main storyline should also be mentioned to give an idea of the depth of the story.

It is also helpful to indicate where you are from time to time.

EXAMPLE: By the end of Act One, Bob Parr decides to give up his boring job as an insurance claims adjuster to return to the excitement and adventure he enjoyed as the superhero "Mr. Incredible." (*The Incredibles*)

This technique lets the executive or producer know you are aware of key plot points and story structure.

Allow for discussion.

Afterwards, allow a few minutes for any questions and comments from the executive or producer. You may be asked and should be prepared to answer the following:

> Do you have a completed script or treatment on this project? (Most potential buyers will not schedule a pitch meeting unless you do.)

> Does your project have any **attachments** (that is, a committed producer, actor or director)? Do not worry if you do not have attachments, as many venues prefer projects with as few encumbrances as possible.

Some buyers play it close to the vest and may not have any comments other than "We'll get back to you." On occasion, some will pass on the spot.

However, if a producer/executive liked your previous work, and if your pitch was well told, you may be asked to contact the producer when your next screenplay is close to completion, even if the project you just pitched does not fit into their present development plans.

This is also the perfect time to ask what is on the studio's or production company's "wish list" of projects. What genre of films are they looking for? If you have a project that might be suitable, it is appropriate to mention it. If the potential buyer has the time, he may even ask you to tell them a little bit about it. But if he does not ask you about the project, do not force the issue.

Be receptive.

In general, be open to all comments and responses given. You might file suggestions in a feedback file.

More specifically, if the same plot point is questioned by different potential buyers, consider reworking and clarifying that particular area of the project.

Do not be surprised if an executive or producer tells you that he or she (or another studio/company) has something similar in development. Similar story ideas seem to come in waves — remember *18 Again, Vice-Versa,* and *Big*? Few people remember the first two films mentioned, but most people fondly remember *Big*, which was released last, but was the most successful of the three "body switch" movies. "Something similar" does not mean someone has "stolen" your idea. "Something similar" can mean a project is set in the same historical period or has a very similar "hook" as your idea.

Be prepared.

If the buyer shows an interest in your pitch, ask if she would like to see the screenplay. If you have not completed your screenplay, give her an idea of when it might be completed.

Legally, the buyer cannot ask a writer for written material without the agent's or entertainment attorney's knowledge, but many writers carry a P.O.P. with them and hand it out at the end of the meeting. Just be sure that your name, your agent's name (if you have one), address, email and phone information are also included.

Since executives and producers hear dozens of pitches each week, they may need a summary to refer to if they want to take further action on your project. Most writers would rather have a potential buyer refer to a summary they have written, rather than to rely on the exec's or producer's memory.

If a buyer is "high" on your pitch and asks to see the script, have a copy available. If you do not have an agent, request a release form (see page 185 for more information on release forms). If you have an agent, call the agent immediately after the meeting and let her know that a script of your project is with John X at Z Films, so your agent can record the information and follow up on it.

Do not give up.

Keep in mind that there is more than one studio or production company around. One rejection does not indicate failure.

If, however, you have pitched your project to several entities without so much as a nibble, you may want to consider shifting the focus of your efforts on your next project and put the first one aside.

Distance and time will sometimes yield new ideas and insights that can improve your initial work.

Remember that a pitch meeting is usually only given to writers whose work has been favorably read. If you are fortunate enough to have obtained a pitch meeting, please make sure that you are well prepared. Because time is at a premium, writers (especially those who are less experienced or "unproduced") may not get another opportunity to pitch to the same person again, unless that initial pitch was exceptionally well told.

With the onset of technology and to address the growing interest in screenwriting around the world, be sure and check Chapter Fifteen for more information on optional ways to get your projects noticed by utilizing the Internet.

For those of you who are eager to test the waters of Hollywood, here are some recommended websites regarding pitching and pitchfests:

The Great American Pitchfest — *pitchfest.com*

Hollywood Pitch Festival — *fadeinonline.com/events/hollywood_pitchfest*

Screenwriting Expo — *screenwritingexpo.com*

PitchQ — *pitchq.com*

Chapter 4

Talking' The Talk: Industry Speak
(aka "What The Hell Are They Talking About?!")

One of my clients from Canada had his first meeting with a production company. I called and asked him how the meeting went. He excitedly told me how the producer and his development director were both dressed in black, and talked about "attaching" something to his script, how the story could be "franchised," and that they needed to know who was "fronting" him and whether there would be enough room for a "back end."

He then paused to ask, "So is this good or bad?"

While you are attending a writer's conference, a pitchfest or a film festival, or perusing the trade papers or anticipating your first Hollywood meeting, you will likely become aware that there are a number of strange-sounding phrases and terms being bantered about. These "buzz words" are peppered throughout the conversations of industry-related personnel. You know they are speaking English, but *what kind*? You are probably overhearing what is commonly called "**industry speak**." No, it is not exactly a foreign language, but it is a language of terms that are common to people who are involved in the day-to-day running of the entertainment industry.

In order to help you fully understand what is going on in Hollywood, as well as keep you one step ahead of many other emerging writers, it is wise to have a working knowledge of some of these phrases and terms. To better acquaint you with them and what they really mean, let us follow a fictitious new screenwriting duo (we will call them Lauren and Joel), who are about to experience their first brush with success in Hollywood. (And let's keep in mind that this could be YOU!)

INT. – ONCE UPON A TIME – THE PRESENT.

JOEL and LAUREN are attending a writer's conference for their very first time. They are almost finished with their script, an exciting adventure project. They feel the timing is right to give Hollywood a try. Because they registered early at the conference, they are given a coveted ten-minute appointment with a well-known PRODUCER.

The Producer asks, "So what's the *log line* on your spec and is it *high concept* or *low concept*? Is it a theatrical film or is it more appropriate as a *MOW*?"

WHAT HE REALLY MEANS IS: "Give me an exciting one- or two-sentence summary (**log line**) on your script (written on "**speculation**," i.e., without pay) and tell me if it's commercial enough for mass audience appeal (**high concept**) or is it a more specialized, narrowly-focused movie that will have a more limited audience appeal (**low concept**)?" The Producer also wants to know if the project being pitched is a traditional theatrical motion picture or a Movie-of-the-Week (**MOW**) meant for television or cable.

Joel and Lauren are prepared with their log line and proceed to pitch their story. The Producer asks for clarification on the hero's *character arc*. Lauren and Joel quickly explain how the main character transforms himself from an ordinary Joe into a courageous and resourceful hero who learns that victory is not about strength of body, but strength of inner resolve. Now the Producer is clearly showing some interest and queries: "So who's getting *story by* and who's getting *written by* credits?

WHAT HE REALLY MEANS IS: "What is the main character trying to achieve, not only physically, but emotionally or spiritually (**character arc**)." and "Did both of you come up with the story and are both of you writing the screenplay, or did one of you come up with the story and the other is going to write the script?" The Producer is trying to establish each person's actual participation in this project. **Story by** simply means who came up with the basic storyline and main characters for the script. **Written by** simply means who is writing the actual script that is based on that story. In addition to clarifying their credits on the screen, each person's participation can often determine the actual division of monies should a project be sold.

After establishing that Joel came up with the storyline and both Joel and Lauren will be writing the script, the Producer asks: "Are there any *attachments*?" Are you registered with *the Guild*?

WHAT'S ACTUALLY BEING ASKED: Is there a director or actor/actress who has agreed to be in this project (**attachment**) if it is set-up with a distributor and/or financing is acquired? The Producer also wants to know if Lauren and Joel have registered their material with the **Writers Guild of America**, which serves as the union representing screenwriters.

Lauren tells the Producer that there are no attachments to their project and that yes, it is registered with the WGA. Lauren would also like the opportunity to direct, to which the Producer comments, "So you're looking to become a *hyphenate*?"

WHAT HE REALLY MEANS IS: "So you're interested in becoming a writer-director?" A **hyphenate** is a person who receives more than one credit on the same project, such as a writer-producer or writer-director. George Lucas of *Star Wars* fame is a writer-producer-director hyphenate. Sandra Bullock is an actress–producer hyphenate on her film, *The Proposal,* and both Mel Gibson and Kevin Costner have an actor-producer-director credit for their respective Oscar-winning films *Braveheart* and *Dances With Wolves.*

Joel quickly chimes in that he is confident that their project has the potential to be turned into a television series if the movie is a success. The Producer, sensing a possible *franchise,* responds with, "Have you already written a *pilot and bible?*"

WHAT HE'S REALLY ASKING IS: "Have you written the first introductory episode (**pilot**) as well as a detailed personality breakdown of the characters, how they relate to one another, the set-up of the series, and what ties them together (**bible**)? A **franchise** is when a project can be spun-off and have more than one application (e.g., television series, video games, amusement park attraction/ride, sequels, etc.).

Unfortunately, Lauren and Joel have not written a pilot or bible for a television series based on their project. The producer expresses his interest in the project as a film, but rather than wait for another month for them to finish writing the screenplay, he asks, "Have you written a *treatment* yet?"

WHAT HE'S REALLY ASKING FOR: A **treatment** is generally a five- to ten-page document which will give the Producer all the major plot points and important details of the project, as well as an indication of the project's general structure and character interactions.

Joel and Lauren just happen to have a treatment with them and hand it to the Producer after first asking for, then signing, a *release form.*

WHAT THEY ASKED FOR: To avoid any possible legal problems, Joel and Lauren know that they need to have a written record that the Producer has seen their treatment. Signing a **release form** protects both the writers and the Producer.

INT. – A FEW DAYS LATER.

The Producer has read the treatment and loves it! He is interested in seeing the script when it is done. Joel and Lauren are having second thoughts and want to submit the material to all the major studios on their own. The Producer tells them, "None of the studios will accept an *unsolicited* piece of work."

WHAT HE REALLY MEANS IS: The studios have strict legal policies that prevent them from accepting material from anyone unless the material is submitted by a producer, agent or entertainment attorney. Material that comes to a studio, agency or production company without representation is considered **unsolicited**. He wants them to understand that if they stick with him, they will have a better chance of having their work accepted.

He asks "Do you two have a *Guild-signatory ten-percenter?*"

WHAT HE'S ASKING IS: "Are Lauren and Joel represented by an agent who is affiliated and approved (a **signatory**) by the Writers Guild of America?" The term **ten-percenter** refers to the 10% commission that agents make when they sell a writer's work.

Joel and Lauren tell the Producer that they do not have an agent yet, but would love to have a referral from the Producer. Eager to maintain his interest in Joel's and Lauren's project, he tells them that he would be happy to place a call to an AGENT he has done business with at a small but respected agency. He tells the Agent that he is interested in the adventure project that they are working on, but they do not have representation. Would the Agent be willing to look at their script and consider *fronting* them on this project?

WHAT HE'S REALLY ASKING IS: Would the Agent do him a favor and look at Joel's and Lauren's screenplay and consider representing (**fronting**) them on this project?

INT. – THREE WEEKS LATER.

Joel and Lauren have finished their script and the Producer has given it to the Agent who agrees to represent them. The Agent thinks, "The project would be better if it were *packaged*."

WHAT HE REALLY MEANS IS: The Agent feels the project could be more desirable to a potential studio if he added a **name** (well-known) director or actor/actress who could bring the project more prestige or appeal. **Packaging** is the process of putting the talent (and oftentimes the financing) together with the script.

The Producer tells the Agent that he will take his chances without packaging the project, but he needs to take the project to Studio A first because he has a *housekeeping deal* with them.

WHAT HE REALLY MEANS IS: He has an arrangement with Studio A. They provide him with an office and a small staff (**housekeeping deal**). In exchange he is required to bring all of his projects to Studio A first before taking them anywhere else. This is also referred to as a **first-look deal**.

Joel's and Lauren's script is sent to Studio A's Story Department for *coverage*, where the story analyst will read and evaluate the project. Nine out of ten of the scripts that cross the reader's desk are a *Pasadena*.

WHAT THIS REALLY MEANS IS: The story analyst will write up a report (**coverage**) that consists of a log line, detailed synopsis and a commentary that is based on factors such as characterization, dialogue, budgeting, pacing, originality of story idea, structure, etc. If the analyst rejects or passes on a project, it is often referred to in unflattering terms as a **Pasadena**.

In this case, Joel's and Lauren's script is given very good marks and the script is shown to the rest of the *creative group*. The Producer knows that unless Act One immediately captures the executives' interest, some of them may resort to the dreaded *30/10 read*.

WHAT THIS REALLY MEANS IS: Joel's and Lauren's screenplay is to be read by the directors of development (or creative execs), vice presidents and senior/executive vice presidents of production (**creative group**) to see if they agree with the analyst's assessment that this project has the potential to be considered for their production development lineup. The Producer knows that if the script doesn't "hook" the executives in the first twenty to thirty pages, the execs will be sorely tempted to simply skip to the concluding ten pages just to see how it ends, leaving a vast majority of the script unread (**30/10 read**).

Studio A asks if the Producer has *optioned* the project or if it was an outright *sale*.

WHAT THIS REALLY MEANS IS: Studio A is merely trying to determine if the Producer put up a fee entitling him to "temporary" exclusive rights to the project for a mutually agreeable period of time (**option**) or if the Producer bought the script "outright" (**sale**)? The Studio wants to know what the legal status of the project is so they can factor in how much money they will need to reimburse the Producer before they become involved in a deal which will ultimately bring them sole ownership rights to the project.

Studio A is not sure it wants to do such a high-budgeted project. The Agent steps in and tells Studio A that Studio B has heard about the project and is eager to do business with the Producer. Studio A feels the *heat* and realizes a *bidding war* may ensue, so they decide to make a quick, lucrative deal at the Agent's suggestion.

WHAT THIS REALLY MEANS IS: When Studio A's interest seemed to waver, the Agent (as a courtesy) let them know of another Studio's interest. This put pressure, intense interest, and focused hype (**heat**) on the project. Studio A did not want to get into a situation where they would be in an escalating financial high-stakes competition (**bidding war**) for Lauren's and Joel's project.

The Studio makes a deal with the Producer and gives Joel and Lauren *$200,000 against $400,000.* The Studio gives the Producer his usual fee plus *points.* The project is then assigned to a creative team of executives who will *shepherd* the script through *development.* The Producer tells Joel and Lauren that he hopes they will not have to go through *Development Hell.*

WHAT THIS REALLY MEANS IS: Joel and Lauren will receive $200,000 for the sale of their script. If the project is produced, they will receive an additional $200,000 for a total deal of $400,000 (**$200,000 against $400,000**). In addition to his usual producer's fee, the Producer, who has produced several successful movies, is given certain percentage **points** if the movie makes a profit. The creative team of a senior/executive vice president and a director of development will guide the project (**shepherd**) as they work with the Producer and the writers to hopefully improve and hone a script through each revision (**development**). Occasionally, egos, budgets and other hard-to-control variables intrude upon the process, making the working relationship very volatile and turning the situation into a negative one (**Development Hell**).

The first set of *development notes* mentions such comments as *Morse Code* and *on-the-nose*, and the *lead shepherd* wonders if the next revision will have to be a *page-oner*.

WHAT'S ACTUALLY BEING SAID IS: The first detailed memo of suggestions (**development notes**) written by the creative team addresses the project's storytelling weakness of giving away too much of the plot in advance (**Morse Code, aka telegraphing the plot**). The notes also mention that the writers have a tendency to write dialogue that explains things in a very obvious manner, and is therefore too **on-the-nose**. The senior or executive vice president of the creative team (**lead shepherd**) is not sure if the writers will have to do a complete revision, starting from the very beginning (**page-oner**).

After a series of revisions the creative group thinks the project is in good enough shape to attach a director or star so that the project can be *greenlighted*. Director X and Actress Z are interested and will have a *pay-or-play* deal with significant *back-end participation*.

WHAT'S REALLY BEING SAID IS: The script is ready to put a Director and Actor/Actress on the project so it can be approved for filming (**greenlighted**). The agents or attorneys for Director X and Actress Z want their clients to have a provision in their contract stating that they will each be paid their full salaries even if the movie is never made (**pay-or-play**). This is a form of insurance policy for the Director and Actor/Actress since their in-demand talent would not be available for other possible offers if they are committed to work on this project. This clause is only given to talent with a history of successful films under their belt. Also, some top-name stars and directors will often negotiate a clause which gives them a percentage of the profits after a film has been released (**back-end participation**).

Studio A tells Joel, Lauren and the Producer that Actress Z brings a lot of *star baggage* to the project that could spell trouble. But the deal is struck and the project is about to go into *preproduction* when the head of production is given an *indie prod deal* and the new head of production puts the project into *turnaround*.

WHAT THIS REALLY MEANS IS: Actress Z wants to throw in a lot of added expenses into her contract, such as specially designed dressing rooms, high-priced hair stylists, makeup artists, fitness trainers, therapists, etc. (**star baggage**). When a project is given the "go ahead" to cast all the characters, find locations, hire a crew, design sets, costumes and props, etc., this is known as **preproduction**. It takes place from the time the script is given the **greenlight** until the time actual filming begins. When the head of production is fired, a studio sometimes pays off the rest of his contract by giving him an independent production deal (**indie prod deal**) which means he can buy and develop films as a producer with a first-look deal on the studio lot. For one reason or another, the new head of production may decide not to go ahead with Joel's and Lauren's project and will put it on inactive status (**turnaround**) in hopes that Studio B or any competitors may want to pay all the costs incurred to buy the project.

As luck would have it, the Agent has contacted Studio B, who is interested in Joel's and Lauren's project. Studio B suggests paying half the costs to Studio A and go into a *co-production* or *joint venture*. Studio A readily agrees to this. Joel's and Lauren's movie makes it to the big screen and is considered *boffo*.

INT. – THE HAPPY ENDING.

Realizing that sharing the costs is much less of a risk, Studio A and Studio B go into partnership together on agreed-upon costs (**co-production** or **joint venture**). Joel's and Lauren's script becomes a film with great box office success (**boffo**).

INT. – A YEAR LATER.

Joel's and Lauren's project was so successful that a major television network is interested in taking their film's major characters and unique situation and turning their project into a television series.

Network XYZ Exec calls Joel and Lauren. She wants them to come to the network offices to meet with Producer J, who is a major *showrunner*. Since their movie was such a box office success, there probably won't be a need for a *back door pilot*, but they would like Joel and Lauren to work closely with the showrunner and his writing staff to come up with a bible as well as a first-episode pilot to make sure the series will have a smooth transition to the small screen.

WHAT'S REALLY BEING SAID: The Exec wants them to meet with a television producer who has a track record of putting together a number of highly successful television series (**showrunner**). He has the confidence of the network and the sponsors to head up Joel's and Lauren's series because he has a very high rate of success in "running new series." Oftentimes, networks will have a ninety-minute or two-hour movie/expanded episode to test whether the project has enough appeal for an audience. In this case, Joel's and Lauren's movie was already very successful, so a **back door pilot** won't be necessary. The network would like Joel and Lauren to work with Producer J and his staff on writing a prototype first episode (pilot) that will start the series off on the right track with a strong, compelling storyline. Because Joel and Lauren created the original characters for the movie, the network and Producer J feel it is important to have the two creators working closely with the writing staff to come up with a series guide (bible) which gives an overview of the series, as well as character breakdowns and an idea of the series' arc for season one and the next few seasons. Most bibles also contain a synopsis or script for a pilot episode or sample episode. If the series gets greenlighted, the bible will be used by the writing staff to assure that they remain true to the characters and the tone/style of the series.

In working with Producer J's staff, Joel and Lauren are told that most of Network XYZ's one-hour dramas have *A-B-C stories*. In addition, Producer J would like each episode to have a *teaser* to introduce the *hook*, four act breaks, and a *tag*. He would like to add a little more humor to the characters, making it more of a *dramedy* instead of a serious drama.

WHAT'S REALLY BEING SAID: Producer J and the Network would like to have one major storyline in each episode (**"A" story**) as well as two slightly less important storylines (**"B" and "C" stories**) to run through each episode. Producer J prefers that each episode open up with a brief opening scene (**teaser**) that will give the audience an intriguing idea of what each week's situation or challenge will be (**hook**) as the opening credits are being run. He would like each episode to end with a brief scene that comes up as the end credits are rolling, which gives the audience an idea of what might be happening next week or what personal insights one of the main characters might be having (**tag**). Producer J's suggestion to add more humor to the characters will make this a merger between a drama and comedy (**dramedy**).

INT. – NINE MONTHS LATER.

The series premieres and after a month's worth of episodes in the *Nielson's Top 10*, the network happily renews the series for the next season. Joel and Lauren, who are learning the ropes as television staff writers on the series, join the rest of the writers and Producer J, who cheerfully makes a champagne toast to "five more years and a *syndication deal* that will bring us all a lot of *residuals*."

WHAT'S REALLY BEING SAID: If Joel's and Lauren's series can continue being an audience favorite (according to the rankings in the **Nielson Ratings**) for at least five or more years, it is very likely that the series can be sold for a very lucrative sum of money to groups of domestic television/cable stations in North American, as well as to foreign markets, for repeat broadcasts ("reruns") of the series (**syndication deal**). **Residuals** are payments made to actors, directors and writers who were involved in creating the television series. They receive a fee or royalty each time the series is shown in reruns.

Chapter 5

Taking The Meeting: What To Do When You Meet The Moguls

A writer was excited about his first meeting with a bigwig at one of the networks. Unfortunately, his appointment was on September 11, 2001, so his meeting had to be rescheduled. Realizing that his project (a one-hour drama series about a crack team of government agents on special assignment) might not be appropriate in light of recent events, the writer changed his drama into an ensemble comedy, which actually interested the exec. Although he eventually turned the series down, the bigwig got the writer another meeting with an important showrunner, who hired the writer as a story editor on one of his hit shows.

Now there's an example of a fast-thinking writer who knew how to be flexible!

INT. — YOUR LIVINGROOM — DAY
The phone RINGS. YOU answer the phone.

> YOUR AGENT
> Guess what? Spielberg just read your latest
> screenplay. He wants to meet with you next
> week.

You collapse to the floor, shaking.

> YOUR AGENT
> Are you still there? Do you wanna take the
> meeting or not?

You pick yourself off the floor.

> YOU
> (being nobody's fool)
> Yes! Of course!!!!

CUT TO

EXT./INT. — AMBLIN ENTERTAINMENT — DAY

You confidently stride from the parking lot into Spielberg's adobe-walled, Santa Fe-style bungalow carrying under your arm the screenplay that you just know will be Spielberg's latest and ultimately best film ever. A cocky smile crosses your face as you enter.

EXT. — AMBLIN ENTERTAINMENT — LATER

SPIELBERG shakes your hand as you are leaving Amblin. You strut away with a multimillion-dollar check in your hand. As Spielberg closes the door, you give a fist pump worthy of Tiger Woods.

FADE OUT

While the scenario above is every scriptwriter's dream, hearing the words "We'd like to meet with you" can send tremors of fear into the hearts of many a writer, novice and veteran alike. Such was the case with an emerging writer I knew. She received a call from an assistant, asking if she could meet with a big-time producer. While she hastily agreed to a meeting with the producer, she realized, after hanging up the phone, that she did not have a clue about what was expected of her at this, her very first "Hollywood" meeting.

If you are fortunate enough to receive a call from a Hollywood professional asking if you would like to "take a meeting," knowing what is ahead can help you prepare — both mentally and emotionally.

Here are some suggestions for what to do when you get your big opportunity to "meet and greet Hollywood."

Gather some background.

First, if you have an agent or manager, ask him to find out how the meeting came about.

> Did a producer or executive read some of your work? If so, which script(s) were read?

> Is the producer taking this meeting at the request of your agent?

> Did the caller specify whether the company is interested in purchasing this screenplay, or is this a request for a "get-acquainted" meeting based on the fact that someone liked your work?

> Is the producer open to hearing new ideas at this meeting?

> If so, does the agent know what is on his or her wish list?

If you do not have an agent, you should still try to track down the source of the request if possible.

> Did you send a recent script or query letter to this producer or exec?

> Did you just win a screenwriting competition or make the finals in a script contest?

> Was this a speaker or presenter you met at a writing conference, pitchfest or industry networking event who may have liked your pitch?

In most cases, the producer or executive requesting the meeting has probably read at least one of your screenplays or heard about your latest script and obviously feels you possess talent. But be forewarned: The meeting may not necessarily signal a sale or option for you. In fact, unless your agent or the person calling you specifically mentions significant interest in your script, chances are a sale or option will not be in the offering.

In all likelihood, the producer or exec may want to find out what other material you have written or are in the process of writing. Perhaps the company or studio has an open writing assignment — either to rewrite an existing project or to write an in-house idea — and your recent submission may be in the same genre or category.

Before the meeting, it would be wise to do some research of your own. Some of the basic information you should gather before-hand includes the following:

> What are the company's most recent credits (both successes and failures)?

> With whom will you be meeting? What is their title? What are their responsibilities?

> Does the company seem to prefer high- or soft-concept projects, or does it seem to produce a mixture of both?

> Does the company produce low-, medium- or high-budget films or films with a wide range of budgets?

> Does the company seem to concentrate on certain movie genres (e.g., dramas, comedies, thrillers, horror, etc.)?

> Do the films seem geared for a specific audience (e.g., children, families, young adult males, women, etc.)?

> Who were the major players in the company's last few productions (e.g., actors, actresses, directors, etc.)?

If the company is a television production house or cable or network entity, you should learn the following information:

> Does the company produce mostly TV or cable series, Movies of the Week, miniseries or specials?

> Is the emphasis on comedies, dramas, animation or children's programming?

> Do any actors/actresses have "deals" with the company?

Why does a writer need to know all of this? Here are just a couple very good reasons for being forearmed:

> You can use much of the information as an icebreaker. All producers and executives enjoy talking about their projects; such a conversation is an excellent way to let them know that you are not only knowledgeable about the industry, but also specifically interested in their production company/studio.

> You can also use what you have learned to help select a couple of appropriate projects (either written or partially written) that might be suitable for their company. That way, if you are asked what you are working on, you will be prepared with a project that is more likely to fit into their general development slate. It is not a bad idea to work on a three- to five-minute pitch, just in case.

Plan the logistics.

If you are coming to the meeting from a considerable distance, you may want to arrive the day before, if possible. Then you will have adequate time to check into your hotel, rest (especially if you are coming from another time zone), and get clear-cut instructions on how to go to the studio or production company.

If you are driving to the meeting, ask hotel personnel how long it may take to reach your destination. Make sure you tell them the time of your appointment. If you are driving to a studio, ask the people you are meeting if you will need a "drive on" pass, which entrance you should use, and where you are supposed to park.

If you are not driving, be sure to pre-order a taxi. Allow extra time so you can arrive at your destination without fear of being late.

If you are coming from out of town and must either fly or drive in and out of the area on the same day, it is best not to schedule your appointment before 11 a.m., if you have a choice. Airports and freeways in Los Angeles County are notoriously congested in the morning. Also, it is not unusual for many producers and execs to start their day with breakfast meetings that keep them out of the office until mid- to late-morning.

If you have a choice, try not to schedule a meeting at the very end of a work day (after 6 p.m.). There are three reasons for this strategy. One is that the typical work day gets busier as the hours stretch on and, by the end of the day, the producer or exec may be more overwhelmed. Second, if any of the meetings scheduled ahead of yours are running late, everything else on that person's agenda will also be running late. And finally, if you have a plane to catch or a dinner appointment to keep, you may also be feeling somewhat restricted and stressed as well.

Last but not least — always call ahead to confirm a meeting.

Look the part.

While there is no formal dress code in Hollywood, it is best to wear neat, presentable, comfortable clothing. For men, slacks or casual pants and a collared shirt are appropriate. Polo-style shirts or short-sleeved shirts are fine. Suits and ties, for the most part, are not really necessary and seldom worn for pitch meetings. For women, slacks or a skirt with a blouse or sweater are fine, as is a casual dress. Shorts, tank tops, sweats or revealing outfits, however — no matter how comfortable — are not the best clothing choice.

Do not forget to bring along a pen and a pad of paper to jot down any notes if you do not trust your memory. Unless you have gotten permission in advance, it is best not to bring along a cassette recorder to the meeting. If you will be pitching a project (or if you think there is a remote possibility you might be), bring along note cards or an outline of your pitch if you think you will need them.

And, remembering the lessons of Chapter Three, you might bring a P.O.P. to leave in case the potential buyer is interested.

Suppress the urge to bring along a camera. Most studios will not allow them on the lot anyway. Also, be aware that once you have entered the gates of the studio, you are on private property. Security personnel can request and legally have the right to look into briefcases, backpacks, purses, and the trunk of your car.

Be prompt, patient, and flexible.

When you arrive at the studio or production company, the receptionist or security personnel will ask your name, the name of the person you are meeting, and the time of your appointment. While it is wise to arrive slightly early or at least on time, do not be surprised if your meeting does not start right on time. It is not uncommon for producers or execs to get tied up in other meetings or stuck on important phone calls. Use the wait to read the trades, which are usually sitting nearby. These newspapers can give you additional up-to-the-minute industry information for "small talk."

While a producer or exec may not have mentioned it, do not be surprised if there is another creative exec or development associate included in your meeting. Usually this person will be responsible for writing up any ideas you may pitch. Producers and executives sometimes schedule multiple meetings a day, and it can be difficult to remember who pitched what when 6 p.m. rolls around.

From a potential buyer's point of view, it is helpful to have another person listening to a pitch, especially if the project being considered is a comedy or is of a very specific genre. What may make you laugh may go over the head of someone else, so with an additional person in the room, the better the chances are that a comedy will be well received. The same is true if a sci-fi, fantasy or unusually complicated project is being discussed. The more "ears" hearing your idea, the better the chances are that your project will appeal to at least one of the two persons receiving your pitch.

Relax and chat.

Most meetings start off with the usual introductory patter: Where do you live? Did you go to film school? How did you get started in writing? Producers/execs will often ask about your favorite movies, hobbies, books, etc. While some of this is "getting to know you," your hosts may file away the information for future reference. And that can pay off:

I once asked a writer what he did in his spare time and discovered he was a baseball fanatic who was an avid participator in fantasy leagues. Several weeks later, my studio was looking for someone to do a rewrite on a baseball project we had in development, and that writer turned out to be the first one we considered for the assignment.

Getting down to business.

There will almost always be a few words about your script. The producer has read it and will probably tell you what she liked most about your story or the writing. If the company is interested in buying or optioning your script, she will usually let you know at the top of the meeting.

If you have an agent, manager or entertainment attorney who represents you, the producer or executive will probably have discussed this possibility in advance. Hopefully your representative has informed you about this likelihood as well. Negotiating, however, is usually done by the agent, and not during your meeting with the buyer. In fact, in most cases, negotiating directly with a writer can be considered "poor form." Most producers or execs would prefer having these discussions with the writer's representative if possible, so as not to "sour" the solid working relationship that must exist, should they be producing your script. This approach is called keeping the deal "pure."

If you do not have an agent, listen carefully to everything that is said. Take notes if you like. Most producers/execs will ask you up-front if you are represented by an agent or an entertainment attorney. Let them know that you are "in the process of finding representation." If you feel comfortable with them by the end of the meeting, you might want to ask if they would be willing to recommend a reputable agent by making a call or letting you use their name as a referral.

Please note that you are under absolutely no obligation to sign with anyone the producer recommends, but it is always worth pursuing a personal recommendation in Hollywood. Such recommendations should not be taken lightly. And remember that having a producer or studio interested in purchasing or optioning your material is a "door opener" for getting an agent to look at your work and possibly represent you.

Use your opportunities.

If the meeting is a "look-see" (most meetings in Hollywood are informational rather than deal-making), and if an opportunity presents itself, you can give a one-minute pitch (an expanded log line) of a project you think might be appropriate for the company or studio. It is up to you to judge whether a genuine opportunity exists.

If you are not certain, you might want to ask the producer or exec if you can schedule a pitch meeting in the near future. If, however, the exec seems interested and asks you to continue, give your three-minute pitch. If the exec is still interested, they will probably ask if you have completed the screenplay. If you have it, you can leave a copy (be sure it is registered with the WGA). If you do not have an agent, you should ask for a release form at this point. If you have an agent, let the potential buyer know that the agency will send a copy of the script, if you do not happen to have one with you.

If the screenplay is not completed, let the exec know what stage it is in — outline, treatment, partial script, etc. — and give a ballpark completion date. It is up to you if you wish to leave a P.O.P. Most writers feel more confident leaving a self-written pitch than relying upon a creative exec to write up his version of your idea.

Do not be afraid to ask what kinds of projects the company is interested in doing or if the studio has development deals with any particular acting or directing talent. This information can prove invaluable to you in the future and gives you an idea of the direction and needs of the company or studio. Asking questions also implies a genuine interest.

Fill in the blanks.

Most look-see and pitch meetings last about half an hour. Once the meeting is completed, take the time for a breather and treat yourself to a cup of tea or coffee. Go over your notes, filling in other details that you feel are important. If you have an agent, give them a call to describe how the meeting went. If you pitched a specific project, left any written material, mentioned a project in the works or promised to send a copy of your material, it is important to inform your agent so they can follow up at the appropriate time.

Some writers keep a log of meetings, recording the day, date, time and place of each appointment, as well as the names of the studio or production company personnel with whom they met. Details of any information gathered from the meeting and the reactions to any projects mentioned or pitched should also be noted. This log can be very helpful in establishing a "paper trail" of your project as well as a "refresher" to remind you of anything that needs follow-up.

Follow-up.

A day or two after the meeting, you may want to send an informal note to the person with whom you met. Thank the producer or exec for meeting with you to discuss your work, and mention the title of the project(s) you pitched or discussed. If the producer or exec was especially helpful (in recommending an agent, suggesting a more appropriate contact for one of your projects, or giving constructive criticism or praise for your work), mention this in your note.

If you told the exec about any work in progress, you can close your note by saying something along these lines: "I'm halfway through my latest thriller, which should be completed within the next month or so. The story has a strong female lead, and since Actress X has a production deal with your company, the script might fit nicely into your development slate." In this way, your "thank you" note serves a dual purpose: to thank the producer or exec, and to give you the opportunity for an invitation for more work and meetings in the future.

If your meeting goes well, it will probably be the first of many. Whether your first meeting results in a sale or not, it can be the start of a potentially productive business relationship.

Chapter 6

Making A List And Checking It Twice: Ten-Point Checklist For A Completed Script

While networking at a screenwriting conference, I met a writer who had just finished her first script. She asked me what she should do next. I started to tell her about my ten-point checklist of questions when her husband, who worked at a Chicago P. R. firm, exclaimed, "Don't worry, honey, I've got that all covered." He handed me a colorful folder containing an 8" x 10" headshot of his wife, a flyer with a mock-up of what her "movie" would look like on a one-sheet, a three-page list of actors, actresses and directors who would be appropriate for the project, along with a bio of his wife which included a list of accomplishments — winner of several beauty pageants, editor of her high school newspaper, the names of several movies in which she had appeared as an extra, etc. He then whisked her off to hand out more of his wife's P. R. packets. Toward the end of the conference, I started to notice a number of those P. R. packets in trash receptacles around the venue.

A week later, I got a phone call from the writer who reintroduced herself and asked, "Now, what exactly was on that ten-point checklist you mentioned?"

You have read all of Linda Seger's books. You have probably taken at least one or two workshops or a couple of courses on screenwriting through your local university or college. You have finally mastered the art of proper margin settings and scene headings. And you have typed, at last, those long-awaited words "FADE OUT," indicating the completion of your script.

Now, take a deep breath and consider your answers to the following important questions before sending your script off to Jerry Bruckheimer, Brian Grazer, or Michael Bay.

1. Are my characters well-drawn and interesting?

Your characters are responsible for telling your story. Along the way, it is vital that they also capture our interest and sympathy. Your hero or heroine should be vulnerable and relatable, as well as courageous. You show these traits by putting your main character through a series of tests in which he or she may sometimes fail but will ultimately succeed.

These tests can be physical and/or emotional in nature and serve as plot complications.

EXAMPLES:

- A septuagenarian overcomes his sorrow and finds the will to live when he shares his sense of adventure with a lonely, well-meaning young wilderness scout in the animated film *Up*.

- Unmarried parents-to-be must put their insecurities aside in a quest to find a place to settle down and to be the best parents they can be in the indie film *Away We Go*.

- A widower overcomes both grief and distance to find love in *Sleepless in Seattle*.

- A Southern belle overcomes her selfish ways, her broken heart, and the horrors of the Civil War in *Gone With The Wind*.

- An ill-tempered ogre learns how to open his heart and finds friendship and love in *Shrek*.

The physical and emotional journey your hero or heroine takes (and the lessons learned along the way) is what is commonly referred to as a **character arc**.

While most writers spend a great deal of time and energy breathing life into their hero or heroine, not nearly enough development goes into their villain and secondary characters. Bad guys and sidekicks are every bit as important as the hero to give your story the texture and tone that can set it apart from all the rest.

EXAMPLES:

▸ Would Captain Kirk and Spock have bonded if they didn't have a common enemy in Nero, who was playing intergalactic cat-and-mouse games with them in *Star Trek*?

▸ Where would Luke Skywalker be without Darth Vader to put him to the test in *Star Wars*?

▸ Would Aladdin have won the love and respect of Jasmine and her father, the Sultan, if he had not defeated the greedy and treacherous Jafar in *Aladdin*?

▸ And who can forget the villainy of Hannibal Lecter, who played a diabolical life-or-death game with Clarice Starling in *Silence of the Lambs*?

Secondary characters give us important backstory on the hero and the situation at hand. They often provide vital information that helps to advance the plot. They help to define the goals of the hero and oftentimes will be involved in a minor subplot that complements and supports the movie's main theme. Secondary characters can also provide comic relief and a contrast to the hero's personality.

EXAMPLES:

▸ Would Ariel still be voiceless without the loyalty of Flounder and Sebastian in *The Little Mermaid*?

▸ Would Harry Potter have been as successful in his quests without the protective friendship of Professor Dumbledore and unconditional support of pals Hermoine and Ron?

▸ Would bridegroom Doug have ever made it from the rooftop of a Las Vegas hotel to his wedding on time if it weren't for his crazy but loyal friends Phil, Stu, and Alan in *The Hangover*?

2. Does my dialogue add to the personality of my characters and support the plot points of my story?

Your dialogue should be meaningful and appropriately "in character" with the personality of each role you have created. It should effectively convey the thoughts and feelings of your characters and reveal any plot points that are key to the progression of the story. All of this should be done, however, in a subtle, natural-sounding way.

Now is the time to go through your script with a mental red pen to make sure each line and each word is absolutely necessary. It is especially important that each character has their own voice. Here are three simple, but effective, ways to test your dialogue:

> Cover up the names above the dialogue and see if each of your characters is easy to distinguish from the others. Remember that your dialogue should be consistent with the personality of each individual.

> Ask your major characters the same question and see if you can give each of them answers that readily separate them from one another.

> Ask members of your writing group or close friends to act out a scene or two. Hearing "lines" spoken out loud can be quite an eye opener for a writer and is a very effective method that can quickly pinpoint any dialogue trouble spots.

3. Does my story fall within a general three-act structure?

Many new scripters are intimidated by the term "three-act structure." Have no fear, writers — all we are talking about is a beginning, a middle, and an ending. All stories (short stories, plays, novels and motion pictures) have the same classic structure. Take a look at the basic three-act structure using the films *Witness* and *Avatar* as examples:

Your "beginning" should have an attention-getting setup that introduces your main characters and their dilemma or situation and who/what stands in the way. By the end of Act One, the hero decides to take on the challenge and plunges into a possible plan of action.

EXAMPLES:

Witness — **Act One.**

Dedicated POLICE OFFICER finds his life in jeopardy when a young AMISH BOY identifies the officer's BOSS as the man behind a drug-related murder.

Avatar — **Act One.**

Paraplegic ex-MARINE becomes part of an Avatar program to infiltrate a supposedly dangerous colony of aliens on a foreign moon.

Your "middle" needs to bring in character dynamics, action and a series of plot complications that both entertain and involve the audience as the story progresses. By the end of Act Two, just when the hero thinks he has everything figured out, there is another seemingly impossible roadblock to face.

EXAMPLES:

Witness — **Act Two.**

The OFFICER is forced to seek refuge in the peaceful Amish community where he is attracted to the recently widowed MOTHER of the young AMISH BOY. The OFFICER finds himself at odds with, but gradually adapts to, the gentle ways of the community. Unfortunately, his BOSS soon discovers his hiding place, putting the Amish community at risk.

Avatar — **Act Two.**

The MARINE is befriended by the blue-skinned aliens who have a deep, spiritual connection to plants, animals and one another. The MARINE falls for a female alien NEYTIRI and realizes that the U.S. military wants to destroy the aliens to obtain a valuable mineral. A battle begins and the MARINE realizes that he must fight for the aliens, who now distrust him.

In Act Three, the hero takes on what seems like the ultimate challenge and is successful in overcoming the odds. Your "ending" should be compelling and satisfying by wrapping up all major and minor plot points and character relationships in a memorable way.

EXAMPLES:

Witness — Act Three.

The OFFICER is confronted at gunpoint by his BOSS and nearly killed, but the Amish community surrounds the two men and "bears witness," forcing the surrender of his BOSS. The OFFICER and the AMISH WIDOW have a bittersweet farewell, knowing their worlds are far too different to compromise.

Avatar — Act Three.

With a few other members of the Avatar team, the MARINE convinces the aliens of his loyalty to them and rallies other alien tribes as they join forces to successfully defend their homeland. The MARINE realizes he belongs with the aliens and keeps his Avatar form to remain with them as their leader, with NEYTIRI at his side.

4. Does each scene have a distinct purpose for being included?

Time to get out that mental red pen again and selectively excise any scenes that are affecting the pace of your story and slowing down your plotline. Many a novice scripter can be easily identified by a screenplay weighed down by extraneous sequences and conversations that go on a beat or two longer than necessary.

If your script weighs in over the unspoken 120-page "line of demarcation," you might want to combine scenes if possible.

EXAMPLES:

▸ Your script contains a series of scenes in which the hero learns two pieces of information. Would your story be just as effective by merging two of the scenes into one?

▸ Your screenplay includes a small scene between the heroine and her mother to show they do not get along. Could that information be included in another conversation your heroine has with her best friend, who already plays a more significant role throughout the overall story?

5. Have I paid attention to details by doing proper research?

If your story is set in a specific area, foreign country or un-usual environment, take the time to read about that location before attempting to recreate it on the page. If your story takes place during a particular historical period, go to the library, surf the Internet or speak at length with an authority on that era for detailed information or interesting anecdotes that can add color and atmosphere. Informa-tion on such subjects as politics, religion, clothing, music, architecture, modes of transportation, women's roles in society, education, issues of the time, etc., can provide valuable observations on what life was like and can add to the challenges of your characters and the conflicts they are facing.

A word of caution, however — try to suppress the urge to go overboard by showing off too much of your newly acquired knowledge. Do not allow those descriptive paragraphs to become so heavily detailed that they overshadow your story and bog down the pace.

If your movie project takes place in an unknown or futuristic world, be sure to take the time to map out the geographical, political, cultural, economical, social, and familial details of this new environment in a concise, stylish manner.

Whether your story takes place in the past, present or future, one of your primary concerns is to immediately immerse your potential buyer or agent into the "world" of your movie project. Familiarizing the reader is what's commonly known as **setting the scene**. The sooner your reader becomes comfortably 'oriented' with your story's surround-ings, the sooner they will be "hooked" into your project.

6. Do I know who my target audience is?

Ideally, all writers would like the whole world to see their movies, but the simple truth remains that not all stories will appeal to everyone. If your goal is to sell your screenplay as a motion picture project, you should find out what other successful films fall into the same category as your script. After finding other movies that fall under the same general genre, you should ask yourself the following:

> What was the predominant age range of the audience viewing those similar films?

> Was it a predominantly male or female audience?

> Did these films have considerable crossover appeal? In other words, did they attract the interest of a wide range of individuals by crossing socioeconomic, racial, cultural, gender and age lines?

> Which studio or production company distributed and/or produced those films? Do you remember how those films were promoted; i.e., what was the emphasis, theme or main thrust of the trailers, television promos and print ads?

It is important to keep in mind that not all movies are meant to be made and distributed by large studios. Many successful films have been made and distributed by smaller independent companies who specialize in less commercial fare.

By knowing who your target audience is, you will have a much more realistic idea of which production companies or distributors to target when you are ready to start submitting your material. If you have not already done so, I urge you to invest in *The Hollywood Creative Directory*. If your local bookstore does not have it, you can contact them at their website: *hcdonline.com*. It contains the addresses, websites, phone and fax numbers of more than 2,500 production companies, networks, cable entities and studios in the entertainment industry.

More importantly, *The Hollywood Creative Directory* contains a partial listing of produced credits and the names and titles of each company's executives. From these listings you can easily eliminate those companies that may not be appropriate for your low-budget horror script or your historical drama, and you will be able to more effectively pinpoint your query by directing it to the appropriate person in charge (usually a creative exec, director of development, story editor or vice president of production).

If your goal is to gain agency representation, you may want to invest in *The Hollywood Representation Directory*, from the same publishers as *The Hollywood Creative Directory*. This directory contains the names, addresses, websites, phone and fax numbers of industry agents and managers. Please pay careful attention to the type of clients each agency or manager represents. Some specialize in representing directors and cinematographers, while others "rep" actors only. Be sure your query goes to an agency or manager who specializes in representing writers.

Needless to say, "targeting" can save a writer considerable time and effort, not to mention the costs of phone calls, postage, envelopes, and duplication of scripts.

7. Have I streamlined my storytelling?

Nothing slows down the reading of a script more than extraneous material. Writers should always focus on writing the best story possible, yet many writers become so involved in detailing their film exactly as they have always envisioned it that they clutter their efforts and end up slowing down the pace of their storytelling. Here are some tips to keep in mind to help you to streamline your script:

> Keep camera angles and descriptive paragraphs to a minimum — even if you are attempting to faithfully adapt a novel. Screenplays of today are lean. They contain very few specific camera angles, and descriptive paragraphs are concise, giving just enough information to set the scene and/or atmosphere.

> Remember to break up any action description so it is not one massive block of words. Describing an action sequence in a series of two or three sentence paragraphs is much easier to read and gives the potential buyer a feeling of anticipation or urgency, as well as movement.

> If possible, eliminate all flashbacks and voice overs or keep them to an absolute minimum. In addition to the extra expense of more sets, props, costumes, actors, etc., flashbacks — if overused and not judiciously placed — can be confusing to the audience.

Voice over is a device that is generally ineffective unless it is used in a highly stylized manner. More recent movies have little or no use of voice overs, although nostalgic film projects can sometimes benefit from a few well-placed voice overs.

Here are some movies where voice overs were used successfully:

> In *The Usual Suspects*, the Kevin Spacey character recalls the details of the crime from his perspective.

> In the film *The Shawshank Redemption*, the Morgan Freeman character gives us an insider's commentary on prison life.

> In the television series *The Wonder Years*, an off-camera adult Kevin sets the scene or conveys his glee, embarrassment or adolescent angst as child Kevin is shown on-camera, acting out the story.

> In the HBO series *Sex and the City*, the heroine Carrie Bradshaw usually has a voice over of the topic of her column, which always ties into the focus or theme of that particular episode.

8. Can I summarize my story in one or two sentences?

When queried by agents or execs, the experienced writer can usually summarize their script with just a few brief sentences, while writers who are less experienced have been known to go on for more than ten minutes or ten pages "summarizing" their movie. To encapsulate the essence of your story, create a "log line," using the steps shown in Chapter Three.

9. Is my screenplay in professional shape for submission?

Much of this information might sound like simple common sense, but form is the one area that can be an overlooked downfall for a novice writer. Here is a checklist:

> All scripts should be cleanly typed or printed. Absolutely no handwritten notations. Remember to use an easy-to-read typeface or font, preferably in 12 point. Times Roman, Courier New, and Arial are the most common fonts used.

> Your screenplay should be carefully proofread for grammatical errors, improper punctuation, and misspelled words and typos. If you belong to a writing group, offer to trade off proofreading duties with another member or ask a friend who excels in English. With every revision of your work, remember to use Spellcheck!

> Be sure your screenplay is copied onto plain white bond. This means absolutely no colored pages, onionskin or parchment.

> You should always submit a copy and never an original of your script.

> Place your script in three-hole punched card stock covers, fastened with two brads that are long enough to hold the script securely. NOTE TO NEW WRITERS: One of the sure signs of a novice writer is putting three brads on your script. Why two brads instead of three? Not having the middle brad makes it easier to turn the pages when reading a script. Remember to use ACCO 1-1/4" brads. Also, most writers use ACCO brad fasteners to keep the brads securely in place. If your local office supply store does not carry the brads and fasteners, order them from The Writers Store (*writersstore.com*). Most screenplays are submitted without a title on the card stock cover, but if you want to have the title printed on the front cover, you may do so. No junior high book report covers, please!

> There should be a title page listing the title of your script and your name as the writer. If you are not represented by an agent, you should put "Registered with the WGA" (if applicable) near the bottom. You should also add an address, phone number and email information so Hollywood knows how to contact you. There is no need to add the registration number or a "warning." If your script is not registered with the Writers Guild of America, I suggest doing so. Registration is currently $20 for nonmembers and the WGA can be reached at the numbers listed at the end of Chapter Two.

> Be sure you have numbered each page of your script in the top right corner. After making copies of your screenplay, be sure to check for any missing pages. Nothing is more frustrating or annoying to a potential buyer (and possibly damaging to your chances for a sale) than coming to an important or crucial part of a story only to find a page or two is missing.

> Be sure you are following the guidelines for submitting a spec or reading script and are not using a shooting script as a template. For detailed guidelines on submitting a spec/reading script, please refer to Chapter Seven.

If you have followed the checklist on the preceding pages, as well as the guidelines for standard screenplay formatting, you should be in good, professional-looking shape. Two of the most reliable references for screenplay formatting are *The Screenwriter's Bible* by David Trottier and *The Hollywood Standard* by Christopher Riley, which can be ordered through The Writers Store (*writersstore.com*). The WGA also puts out a brief, concise pamphlet on formatting. You can contact the WGA for details on obtaining this helpful booklet (*wga.org*).

10. Is this a story that I love?

My advice to new writers is to make your script a story that you love. It does not have to be a story that is commercial, but it should be well written. Few writers sell their first script, but the first few scripts can signal an agent that you are a writer who is consistent, determined, and passionate.

In speaking with scores of successful screenwriters through the years, I have discovered that it takes an average of seven to eight scripts before a writer obtains their first agent or has their work optioned or purchased. Only one writer I spoke to sold her very first script and she was quick to add that it took her five more years before she had another sale. Another screenwriter wrote fifteen scripts before he got an option. He confided, in hindsight, that his first ten screenplays are now an embarrassment to him, but were necessary practice.

It is also important that new scripters understand that most potential buyers are looking at screenplays with two key questions in mind:

> Is this a project that is appropriate for my company?

> Is this a writer that warrants a spot on my "Writers List" for future projects and rewrites?

Many times I have read a screenplay that was not appropriate for the studio where I was employed, but the writing was so impressive that I put the writer on a list for upcoming open writing assignments.

Keep in mind that each of your screenplays should be a labor of love that exhibits strong writing and storytelling skills. That effort can translate into a "calling card" script that will open the doors for future work.

Some words of wisdom: Once you have completed a script, immediately suppress the urge to rest on your laurels. After a congratulatory sip of champagne or designer water, get to work on your next screenplay. Agents and production execs just love doing business with fast, prolific, creative talent!

Chapter 7

The Submission And Development Processes: What Happens To A Script Once It's Submitted

(aka "Who Is Reading My Script And What Are They Looking For?")

While working at Disney, one of the vice presidents had me come by his office to pick up a "hot new script" that an agent had just given him on a "confidential/exclusive" basis. I had to read it overnight and write up a report so he could give the agent an answer by 10 a.m. the next morning. The script was full of logic loopholes, under-developed/superficial characters, on-the-nose dialogue and a storyline that would require a mega-budget. I turned in my report and the vice president, needless to say, was not happy to see a bottom-line "pass." He got into a ten-minute discussion with me and asked if I was "absolutely sure" about my assessment. I stuck to my guns.

A few days later, the VP's assistant told my assistant that the writer of the script turned out to be a former roommate of the agent and that the "confidential/exclusive" submission was also given to four other studio execs. The VP told his assistant he was relieved I had passed on the script after he realized the agent had tried to pull a fast one for a very untalented friend.

Not much gets past us gatekeepers!

Undiscovered scripters are always wondering, "What happens to my screenplay once it is submitted?" Contrary to popular belief, screenplays do not fall into a "black hole." But the submission process — often long and tedious — can try the souls of even the most patient of writers. Let's walk through the typical submission process.

At the start.

If you have a Writers Guild of America-approved agent, he will submit your script to an independent production company or studio. Most major production companies and studios have very strict submission policies, controlled by their legal departments, for all screenplays, teleplays, treatments, novels, and other submitted materials. In most cases, they will accept material only from a WGA-accredited agent, a producer with a viable track record, or an entertainment attorney. Unsolicited material is generally *verboten*.

As mentioned previously, non-represented writers have been known to persuade a smaller independent production company to look at their scripts after they have agreed to sign a release form. (See page 185 for an in-depth explanation of these forms.)

Unless you have a contact who has expressed interest in the project at a particular studio, concentrate on finding a home for their script with a production company. Generally, producers are more willing to champion a project. In addition, if a screenplay has been submitted to a studio in recent years, the chances are good that there is a record of the submission, along with the coverage on it. Accordingly, producers will usually query a writer to find out if he has had the screenplay submitted to the studio beforehand. If it has been submitted to Studio X, the project is likely to be dismissed out of hand even if it has been revised.

Here is another very good reason why you should find a home for your project with a producer. Studios know that producers have taken the time to sift through hundreds of scripts before finding just the right project. They realize that the producer has a vested interest in the script and, more importantly, has most likely established a good working relationship with the writer.

The "Log-In."

Once your screenplay reaches a producer or studio executive, it is likely that he will give it to the story department for what is commonly referred to as the **log-in** — the producer's or studio's legal record of material which has been submitted. All available information is recorded: the title of the project; the writer's name; whether or not the material is based on previous material (i.e., a book, article, play, etc.); the name of the agent, entertainment attorney or producer submitting/representing the project; what form of material (script, book, treatment, etc.); the page count; the date the material is received; and the name of the production company or studio personnel to whom the project is submitted.

The story department will then check its files to see if the material has ever been submitted and evaluated previously. Story department files often go back decades in time. With the advent of computer programs, it is very easy to crosscheck a project, not only by title, but also by the author's name. It is not unusual for writers or agents to change the title of a screenplay in hopes of receiving "new" coverage. Generally speaking, if a project received previous coverage, the story department will send that coverage to the exec. It is then up to the exec to decide if new coverage is warranted.

Some possible factors which may warrant that new coverage be given include: a significant difference in the page count from the original material (usually indicative that more than cosmetic or minor changes have been made), a letter from the producer or agent that indicates a totally new approach to the project, or an indication from the producer or agent that a major director or actor is now attached to the project.

The "Gatekeepers."

In most cases, your script goes to a **reader** or **story analyst** whose job is to thoroughly read and evaluate your project. One studio head has described story analysts as the "gatekeepers."

Although it may sound unkind, producer and studio execs do not have sufficient time to read each and every piece of material that is submitted to them. In fact, at the most, execs will only read submissions from writers who have a track record in the industry or whose work is submitted by a high-profile producer.

This process may seem unfair, but the average studio receives between 800 to 1,000 screenplays every month from agents, producers and entertainment attorneys — not including a large number of unsolicited projects that are generally returned by the mail room and never reach the desk of a studio exec or the story department. It would be virtually impossible for a handful of executives to read and evaluate all unsolicited material and still have time to work with writers on developing purchased scripts while shepherding dozens of projects through the never-ending production pipeline.

If your material is submitted to a studio, it will be read by a story analyst who belongs to the Story Analysts Guild, which is now under the umbrella of the larger Film Editors Guild. In general, union story analysts are better paid and enjoy better benefits than their freelance brethren who usually work for the production companies and agencies. It is not unusual for freelance readers to work for more than two or three production companies to earn a livable salary. Most agency readers, however, are not allowed to work for other production companies or agencies.

Readers who work for agencies are usually planning to move up and become agents and producers. Analysts at the studios are occasionally promoted to become part of the creative group that makes the decisions on which films will be developed and produced. Readers for production companies often use their position as a stepping stone to move up to become part of the company's production staff.

Story analysts/readers vary in skills and abilities, but all are required to read, evaluate and write up a report, called **coverage**, on submitted material. More experienced union story analysts are often called upon to do **development notes**, which are detailed comments and specific suggestions for projects the company has already optioned or purchased. And there is a small cadre of story analysts who are sometimes called upon to do "legal comparisons" in connection with a potential or pending lawsuit. A very small number of story analysts are also trained to do translations of foreign-language scripts.

Both union and non-union readers are occasionally requested to sit in on pitch meetings where they are to take notes and write up a brief summary of the pitch. Readers often do more than simply read. Some are also asked to watch and evaluate student films and director's reels or films submitted for acquisition and distribution. Again, a synopsis and brief commentary is written up and serves as a report to executives who were unable to attend the screening.

A reader's crystal ball.

What do story analysts, producers or studio execs look for in scripts? First, they look for projects they would like to make that would be appropriate for their studio or company. Second, they assess if the writer demonstrates strong enough storytelling skills and is someone they may want to do business with in the future.

In general, studios and production companies rely upon story analysts to look for the following:

> An unusually compelling basic plot that will fit into and balance the company's or studio's existing development slate.

> A project that has a certain amount of commercial potential that will attract a fairly large number of moviegoers.

> Riveting, unique character dynamics that will attract a wealth of casting possibilities.

> Fresh, insightful dialogue that adds to the backstory and the personality of the characters while moving the storyline along.

> A keen visual and emotional storytelling style that can be "seen" and "felt" while the analyst is reading the material.

> The potential for a project that would be appropriate for any directors or acting talent who have a strong connection with the studio or production company.

> A project that might have the possibility of translating into a television/cable series or another potential franchise (video games, theme park rides, Broadway musicals, etc.)

> An exceptionally talented writer who can be put on the Writers List for possible rewrites or to write a script from scratch based on an in-house idea.

The coverage report.

Coverage is a shorthand report that is an essential tool in this highly competitive but lucrative marketplace. Coverage gives the time-conscious executive a concise, accurate (albeit, sometimes sterile) retelling of the main storyline and subplots, accompanied by comments on the material and writing style. The average coverage is usually one- to three-pages in length.

After reading your material, analysts will write a log line followed by a synopsis of the storyline, noting major characters and plot points. Synopses can be as brief as a couple of paragraphs or as long and detailed as prescribed by the producer or studio executive.

The synopsis is usually followed by a commentary detailing the material's strengths and weaknesses, with additional remarks about the writer's abilities and writing style, and reasons why the story did or did not work. Finally, there is an evaluation: "Pass," "Consider" or "Recommend." Many studios/production companies also have "box scores" that rate various aspects of the material, such as premise, storyline, structure, characterization, dialogue, etc. A box score can range between "excellent," "very good," "fair," and "poor."

Short coverage is usually a one- to one-and-a-half page synopsis with commentary. **Long coverage** is much more detailed and usually consists of more than three pages of synopsis and commentary. Long coverage is sometimes requested, especially if the analyst is evaluating a novel. If the material is being covered for an agency or for a production company whose principal is an actor or director, it is not unusual for the reader to also do what is commonly referred to as a "character breakdown."

Character breakdowns generally accompany a detailed synopsis and commentary and also contain a list of the major roles with descriptions noting age range, physical aspects, personality, character arcs, interaction with other characters, and any significant traits that would give the studio exec, production exec or agent a better idea of the casting possibilities.

Coverages of screenplays, novels, pitches, films and other materials also serve as an accurate accounting of what, where, when, and to whom the project was submitted, should a lawsuit arise.

The executive suite.

Readers will then return the submitted material, along with the completed coverage, to the story department. The department will note the date the coverage has been turned in. The material and coverage are then sent to the executive or producer who originally requested the coverage. They, in turn, will read the report. Even if the rating is a "Pass," some producers and execs will read sections of the script if the log line interests them. If your material gets a "Consider" or "Recommend," they will definitely read the script.

If it's a "Thumbs Up."

After the producer or exec reads the material and agrees with a "Consider" or "Recommend," they will present the material to others in the creative group for consideration. If the majority of responses are favorable, the original exec will check the company's development slate to see if the project will fit in — determining whether a company has too many projects in a particular genre and whether the project will meet the company's budgetary guidelines and marketing focus.

At a studio, marketing execs are occasionally asked for their opinions regarding the box office outlook for the potential new project. They will look at the possible demographics, the commercial potential, and ease of selling the project to the public. It is not uncommon for executives from the areas of casting and budgeting to also be called in to read the screenplay and give their opinions.

If the script meets the company's various criteria, a writer's agent or the producer who submitted the project will be contacted and the arduous process of negotiating either an outright sale or an option will begin. If the material was submitted to a production company, the producer will contact the writer and his agent. If the writer does not have an agent, it is strongly suggested that he secure the services of an entertainment attorney and/or an agent to handle the negotiations at this point.

If it's a "Thumbs Down."

If the story analyst's recommendation is to pass on your material and the producer or exec agrees with the assessment after reading the report, your agent or the submitting producer will be contacted (usually by phone). At some companies, the actual material will be returned to the submitter. But with Hollywood being in an ecological mind-set, the script will usually be put in a bin for shredding unless the submitting party specifically requests the return of the material.

A notation will be made by the story department regarding the date the script was returned to the submitter.

The "Positive Pass."

If a reader gives your script a "Pass," but is impressed by the quality and style of your writing, the producer or studio exec will usually read the screenplay. If she likes your writing style, she will be more than willing to continue receiving material written by you and will give serious consideration to hiring you for appropriate polishes, rewrites or new idea assignments — thus the term "Positive Pass." A call will be placed to your agent, who will ask that you be kept in mind as a "writer for hire" on any upcoming projects or rewrites. Many writers have initially established themselves by polishing or rewriting material written by another writer or by writing a script based upon a producer's or studio's in-house idea.

The waiting game.

Do not be discouraged if Paramount or Universal has not called your agent or producer with an immediate response. So much material is submitted to each production company and studio that it can take anywhere from one to six weeks for submission turnarounds. On rare occasions, it can even take up to two months, depending upon the backlog.

Major studios usually have staffs of from six to twelve story analysts who read an average of seven to ten screenplays a week. Production companies and agencies usually have a smaller reading staff. You can do the math, but obviously it can sometimes take a month or more for submissions to be covered. Producers/execs will sometimes ask that a submission receive **rush coverage**, which means they would like the material to be covered immediately (usually within twenty-four hours). Other times they may request **priority coverage**, which means within the next few days.

Rush or priority status is usually given to projects that are "hot" (the submitting agent or the producer is distributing the material to several entities at once) or are written by a scriptwriter who has had several successful produced films under his belt.

The creative group.

As mentioned above, the decisions about purchasing or optioning material is put in the hands of the creative group. This group was first discussed on page 12. At its top is the head of the motion picture division of the studio. At a production company, it is the principal/owner of the company. Immediately under the head of the motion picture group would be the senior or executive vice president of production. At a studio, there are at least one or two persons at this level. At a production company, there is usually only one.

Under the senior or executive vice presidents of production will be the vice presidents of production. At a studio, there are at least two or three at this position. In a production company, there is usually only one. The directors of development (aka "creative execs") are next in line. There are generally three or four execs at this level of the creative group. Some studios and production companies have a story editor whose job is to supervise the readers/story analysts and facilitate the influx of work that flows between the executives and the gatekeepers. Some story editors are also asked for their input as part of the creative group.

The higher up you are in the creative group, the more responsibilities you have and the more weight your opinion is given in determining the fate of a project.

The development process.

Once a script has been purchased, creative execs/directors of development are responsible for gathering up the group's notes and comments and putting them into a document that will be given to the producer and writer for discussion before the next revision of the screenplay begins. In addition to merging the thoughts of the creative group into a readable document. These development executives are also responsible for making sure the notes are not only clear and concise, but also nicely stated so as not to upset any egos.

After a rough draft of the studio notes are assembled, one of the vice presidents or the senior or executive vice president who is assigned to the project will go over the notes and will edit them, if needed. The notes are then sent to the producer and writer and the first of several development meetings will be set.

The development process.

Producers and writers have been known to call the whole process of constant notes, meetings and revisions "Development Hell." In the 1980s (when development was first utilized), there was a tendency to micromanage each project and revision. It was not unheard of for development memos to sometimes exceed ten to fifteen pages. Nowadays, development documents are usually in the two- to five-page range.

After the producer and writer have had a chance to digest the notes from the studio, they decide which points they do and do not agree with. They will often work out an alternate solution and present it to the studio's development team (the director of development and the vice president).

While every writer wants to defend their material (as is well within their rights), most also realize that compromises are usually in order. Here are some of the reasons why the studio may request changes:

> They need to change certain aspects of the plot to keep the project within a reasonable budget.

> They are concerned with straying into an undesirable "ratings" area.

94

> They are concerned with offending or alienating a segment of the moviegoing public.

> They are trying to "woo" a particular star and would like the character and/or storyline to be adjusted to the star's acting range.

> They are trying to attract a particular director and would like the script to be more in line with the director's talents.

> They are concerned about more common issues such as pacing, tightening up the plot, providing dialogue that more strongly supports the character's personality and intent, and making sure to enhance, but balance, all aspects of the project to make it as entertaining and attractive to potential moviegoers as possible.

Some projects only require one or two revisions, while others have been known to go through a dozen or more, as well as several different writers. Contrary to popular belief, most producers and studios would actually prefer to keep the original writer on the project, but if, after a couple of revisions, the writer is unable to deliver a screenplay that is suitable, hiring another writer is sometimes the only possible solution.

This process seems rather unfair, but once a studio or a producer has purchased your script, it is legally in their possession and ownership; they are well within their rights to assign a new writer if they feel they need to do so. Studios and producers do not assign new writers capriciously. Keep in mind that with relatively few exceptions, you (as the writer of the original material) will still receive a writing credit should the project be produced. It may not, however, be a sole writing credit.

"Redlight" moments.

Once a project is bought by a production company or studio, the goal is to give the project a "greenlight" and have it produced. Yet more than half of the screenplays that are purchased do not end up on the big screen. This fact is one of the most puzzling and frustrating aspects of the film industry. Here are some possible reasons why a film may be "abandoned" (dumped altogether) or put into "turnaround":

> A big name actor or actress has decided not to do the project.

> A director has gotten another prime project he would rather do first.

> There has been a major change in upper management.

> The original executive who championed the project has found another position at an opposing company or has been let go in a management shake-up.

> There are other projects coming out from other networks or studios on the same subject or with a hook that is very similar.

> The studio feels that the project's window of opportunity has passed in terms of public interest.

But, as mentioned in Chapter Two, members of the Writers Guild of America now have the right to re-acquire their work.

Submitting for network television and cable venues.

As is the case with writing and submitting material for feature or cable movies, it's important to know who the players are when you want to break into writing for television/cable, or want to pitch a proposal for a series.

A word of caution: No matter how wonderful your series proposal may be, if you do not have previous produced credits, the network or cable entity is not going to take a chance and let you run your own series. The best opportunity they might be able to give you (if they really love your series) is to try and pair you with an experienced showrunner. If that showrunner shares that same avid interest and wants to take on the series, more than likely you will have to be content with a shared "created by" credit and an opportunity to start as a staff writer.

In speaking with several successful staff television/cable writers, many have found that starting at the bottom gives them the insightful perspective and sound working knowledge they need in order to know how a series is created, developed, produced and sustained. Working your way up also sharpens your instincts, expands your network of contacts, and, when combined with your experience, provides a credible backup to a terrific series proposal. More importantly, working on staff is invaluable for gaining the respect of those at the network/cable venues, as well as your fellow writers, so that when you (or they) come up with a killer premise for a series, you will be able to get the series proposal into the right hands.

One question I am frequently asked is why there are so many more writing credits for a television or cable series than for a motion picture. Who are all those writers and what are their responsibilities?

Network and cable series writing positions.

Freelancer — Freelancers are writers-for-hire. They usually do not participate in story meetings. However, this is how a lot of writers are able to get on staff. Maybe a senior writer or showrunner has read one of your spec teleplays, or has heard about your work from other writers on staff or from a network exec. Many times a freelancer is called in to come up with episodic concepts, do a polish on a script, or to do a complete rewrite. On very rare occasions, it's to do a full script.

Staff Writer — This credit usually means you are a first season writer on staff. Your time will be spent writing dozens and dozens of concepts for series episodes. You will also do some rewriting of scripts that may have been started by one of the senior writers on staff. If you are asked to write an episode, it will be under the close supervision of a senior writer and it may or may not be from a concept you initiated.

Story Editor — Usually a second season (or above) staff writer who has been credited with writing at least a couple of episodes will graduate to a story editor. At this point, you will do a lot of major rewriting and the chances are good you can be counted on to write at least one or more episodes of your own during the season.

Executive Story Editor — Generally speaking, this credit indicates that you have more experience than a story editor and are starting to supervise some of the staff writers.

Producer — Writers with this title have produced credits and more experience. You will probably supervise story editors, staff writers and freelancers. Usually producers help to shape the upcoming season and are counted on to maintain the quality of the episodes. Producers are often on-set and may be asked to do last-minute rewrites. Writers at this level are often able to create an original series, sometimes in conjunction with a showrunner, or on their own. This credit is not to be confused with that of a line producer, who takes care of supervising physical production.

Supervising Producer — With this title, a high-level writer in this capacity might run the Writers Room and supervise the writing staff. Oftentimes, this is the person the showrunner will count on to find new staff writers or freelancers for rewrites or polishes. I have been told that it is often the supervising producer who will end up being the person who will tell you if you are hired or fired.

Executive Producer — As the top writer-producer of a series, you will be responsible for supervising and overseeing the entire writing staff, as well as the cast and, occasionally, the crew. Although you will not see the actual title of "showrunner" on the screen, if you see the title of executive producer, it means the same thing. Executive producers determine the course of the series and supervise all creative aspects of the series. Sometimes the showrunner may have created the series, but may not necessarily still write episodes for the series. This is especially true if the showrunner has also created another series in production at the same time. It is not unusual to have more than one executive producer on a series. Oftentimes they will split duties by trading off, either supervising the writers or the cast/crew and network-related responsibilities. Shows with a large cast and multiple storylines (think *Lost* or franchises like *CSI, Law & Order* or *Grey's Anatomy*) are known to have more than one executive producer to accommodate their prolific creators and more complex characters and storylines.

Executive Suite — cable and network television.

Here is a rundown on key execs for the creative group for cable and network television:

Development/Creative Executive — This exec is the person responsible for reading each version of a project, doing comparisons and writing notes on areas of concern. Usually they will take the notes from senior execs and merge them with their notes and discuss them with the series' supervising producer or producer. Development execs also are responsible for bringing attention to any "Broadcast Standards and Practices" problems that may not be appropriate for the time slot or the network or cable venue's policies. Some of those issues could be language, sexual content, or inappropriate storylines.

Vice President — This is a senior exec who is assigned to the series as the liaison and oversees the series from the network/cable end. They also supervise and work with the development exec who is assigned to a particular series and deals with the more important issues that may arise on the show, usually problems on set.

Executive/Senior Vice President — Whether the title is executive or senior vice president, this is the exec who oversees the creative and business end of all of the series for the network or cable venue on a day-to-day basis.

President — This is the head of the creative and business end of things for the network or cable entity. In many respects, the president is the "face" of that company — the person responsible for guiding the executive staff in making decisions involving programming, demographics, and policies that can affect the ratings and the future of the network.

On the subject of ratings and demographics, this is another important arena in television and cable that writers should be aware of.

What are demographics?

"Demographics" or 'demographic data' refers to selected population characteristics that can be utilized by marketing. For network/

cable, age, and gender are the two most important demographics of concern. Sponsors and networks love it when a project can appeal to both male and female viewers, as well as both younger and older audiences.

Why should a TV writer be concerned about demographics?

As with writing for feature films, writers in network or cable TV need to know who the audience is. In other words, who are they writing for? Before you start writing a spec episode for one of your favorite shows, you need to know who is watching that show. Is the audience mostly male or female? What is the age range of the average viewer?

One of the most unproductive things a struggling writer can do is to write a spec episode on a minor character or an issue that is of little interest to the main demographic audience. Likewise, it would not make much sense to write a proposal for a new television or cable series that features a lead character who is a conservative, white-collar businessman, married with young children, if a majority of the demographic audience for that network is single and between the ages of eighteen and twenty-four.

What are ratings? How are ratings and demographics useful to a writer?

"Ratings" are the audience measurement system that determines the audience size and profile for television/cable programming. In the U.S. and Canada, the Nielsen Ratings System is used. Ratings are a statistical method to help television and cable programmers and advertisers in targeting audiences and markets. Ratings are currently the single most important element in determining advertising rates, program scheduling, and program content.

As a writer, if you want to know who the audience is for a particular television series, you can probably determine that audience by looking at the advertisers who run their commercials during that show.

The largest audience (which also means the most expensive commercial revenues) happens during **primetime**, between the hours of 8 p.m. and 11 p.m. Within this three-hour time frame, most network/cable programming is divided up as follows:

8 p.m. – 9 p.m. — Cable and network entities schedule more family-oriented comedies and dramas. Examples include series like *How I Met Your Mother*, *Ugly Betty* and *The Secret Life of an American Teenager*.

9 p.m. – 10 p.m. — Slightly more sophisticated comedies and more intense dramas are usually programmed into this time slot. Examples include *Two and a Half Men*, *The Office*, *30 Rock* and *Grey's Anatomy*.

10 p.m. – 11 p.m. — The most intense dramas and very sophisticated adult comedies/dramedies are scheduled during this hour. Examples include *CSI*, *The Good Wife*, *Entourage*, *Private Practice*, *Burn Notice*, *In Plain Sight*, *Weeds*, *Law & Order* and *Californication*.

Network and cable station programmers have to walk a tight-rope when it comes to pleasing the television public, the producers *and* the advertisers. But as most of you probably already know, the bottom line is that ratings and revenue from advertisers are what keep the networks and cable companies going, so a writer should always keep demographics and ratings in mind when creating a spec episode or new series.

After demographics and ratings, networks and cable companies are interested in the genre of a series. While all execs want "something new," I am sure you have made the same observation I have — while sometimes comedies rule the top of the ratings charts, inevitably dramas will take their place for another several years, and this flips back and forth according to the tastes of the TV-viewing audience. But with the exception of reality, game or news shows, most television series seem to fall into one of several variations of comedies and dramas:

Comedies

Teen — *Hannah Montana*, *The Suite Life of Zack & Cody*, *Wizards of Waverly Place*.

Family — *Modern Family*, *How I Met Your Mother*, *Rules of Engagement*, *Ugly Betty*.

Adult — *Cougar Town*, *Two and a Half Men*, *The Office*, *30 Rock*.

Dramas

Police — The *CSI* and *Law & Order* franchises, *The Closer*, *NYPD Blue*.

Mystery — *Castle, Bones, Burn Notice, Monk*.

Medical — *Grey's Anatomy, Private Practice, House, E.R.*

Family — *Brothers & Sisters, Gilmore Girls, The Secret Life of an American Teenager*.

Teen — *Gossip Girl, 90210, High Society, Melrose Place*.

Courtroom — *JAG, NCIS, Boston Legal, Damages*.

Adult — *Californication, Desperate Housewives, Brothers & Sisters, The Good Wife*.

Fantasy — *Smallville, Deadwood, Supernatural, Vampire Diaries, Heroes, True Blood, Buffy the Vampire Slayer*.

Spiritual/Paranormal — *The Mentalist, Ghost Whisperer, Medium, Joan of Arcadia*.

War-Related — *The Guard, The Unit, Pacific, Band of Brothers*.

Political — *24, The West Wing, La Femme Nikita*.

Sci-Fi — the *Star Trek* franchise, *Babylon 5, Battlestar Galactica, Dr. Who, V*.

For more specific information on the craft of writing for network television and cable, I would like to recommend that you check out the following helpful books: *The TV Writer's Workbook: A Creative Approach To Television Scripts* by Ellen Sandler; *Elephant Bucks* by Sheldon Bull; *Writing The TV Drama Series* by Pamela Douglas.

Chapter 8

Beware Of The Big Nine: The Nine Most Common Reasons Why Scripts Are Rejected

Found this story on the Internet: Seems a screenwriter wrote a comedic screenplay that evidently never caught fire in Hollywood and had been soundly rejected. One of his favorite scenes in his script is when a trailer-trash couple's wedding is interrupted by three strangers who show up to kidnap the bride. When the groom tries to save her, there is a shoot-out. He loved that scene so much that he somehow convinced three of his good friends and his bride to re-enact it, much to the delightful howls and applause of all the guests at their wedding reception!

Now that has got to take the prize for the most interesting but creative way to deal with Tinseltown rejection!

An all-too-familiar discussion took place just recently while "doing lunch" with some of my industry colleagues. As we talked about the ever-crowded script market, our laments over the dearth of really good material seemed to fall into several areas of very similar complaints. Although there is a common misconception among writers that everyone in Hollywood only wants to say "No" to everything, I am here to unequivocally tell you that most of us would prefer — actually, would *love* — to say "Yes!"

Aside from wanting an agent or producer to look at a writer's work, one of the most frequent questions I hear from scripters is: "Why are so many scripts rejected by Hollywood?"

This prompted me to ask other executives, agents and producers about their observations on why nine out of ten submissions fail to even make the "first cut" past story analysts or readers. After an informal survey, it became quite apparent that the reasons for a "Pass" seemed to fall into nine general categories. Let's focus in on what I call "The Big Nine."

1. The Snail Trail/Tangled Yarn Start.

Nothing stops a producer or studio exec faster than a script that fails to move within the initial fifteen to twenty pages. Some writers become so determined to introduce their characters or go into very elaborate detail to describe the location that they fail to hook the audience into the heart of their story by firmly establishing the plot in Act One.

Alas, the reverse is also true. If the movie has too many confusing and tangled pieces of plotting thrown into Act One, an audience will become restless and start asking too many unnecessary internal questions, losing the main thrust of the storyline.

A studio or a production exec faced with a mountain of scripts to read will be sorely tempted to stop reading if Act One is either too plodding or too confusing. One result: the "30/10 read," discussed on page 54. And I am sorry to report that, as submissions are on the increase, several of my colleagues have confessed that they have found it necessary to further streamline things down to a "10/10 read."

While studio story analysts are required to read every page of submitted material per studio policy, that "every page" policy does not always extend to studio execs or freelance readers at production companies. This situation can be disconcerting to a writer, especially if the rest of their project has all the prerequisites for a potentially good script.

2. The Act Two Drag (aka The Mid-Story Sag).

The most common plotting pitfall is allowing the pacing in Act Two to slow to a near halt. Most writers have carefully crafted their attention-getting setup and have envisioned the spellbinding climax to their film, but often fail to give just as much thought and consideration to the story that falls in between the beginning and the end. This problem is especially noticeable in action, adventure, thriller, or "on the road" tales where writers have been known to resort to a series of unimaginative, non-stop chase sequences or a montage of scenery shots or special effects imagery in order to fill the void, show the passage of time, and move their story along.

Unfortunately, the opposite effect seems to take place. The audience loses interest because they are not being given enough essential time investment in the hero's struggle to reach their ultimate goal. And in many cases, the challenges the protagonist faces are not sufficiently laid out to give Act Two a feeling of escalating danger, excitement or jeopardy. As a result, Act Two unexpectedly becomes a huge lull.

It is up to you, the writer, to make sure that Act Two is infused with as much creative style and plotting as you have invested in your dynamite set-up and ending payoff. Act Two is the best time for your audience to get to know your characters and, in turn, to support your protagonist's final goal. This act is also the ideal place to add motivation and backstory, two very subtle but key ingredients in giving your audience a protagonist they can root for. This "root-ability factor" gives the audience an emotional investment in your main characters. Every scene in Act Two should build in intensity and importance, and serve to catapult the audience toward your Act Three climax.

3. The Frenzied Finish.

Many writers toil through their scripts, only to suddenly panic when they realize that they have arrived at page 100. Frantically, there is a mad dash to provide a non-stop finish for the very final fade out. One common example of what I call "the frenzied finish" is the **explanatory ending**, where the hero sits everyone down and starts to explain everything — who, what, why, where, when, and how. While this technique may be used with some degree of success in occasional television series of the past such as *Murder She Wrote* or *Diagnosis: Murder*, it seldom works for cable, network television or theatrical movies.

A movie's ending should never feel rushed or contrived. The climax should always be satisfying. All plot points and character relationships should be resolved in a logical and, hopefully, entertaining fashion. And although you want to keep your audience guessing, no one appreciates a story where the ultimate villain or his underlying motive seems to come out of left field without an adequate set-up beforehand to support and justify the final outcome.

Take sufficient care with Act Three. Although it is usually somewhat shorter in page length than Acts One and Two, your third act's final dozen or so scenes will leave the most lasting impression on your audience. And that last impression could generate either good or bad "word of mouth" on your movie. It is even more crucial to create a memorable and satisfying ending on the *reading* pages of the script or it may never be able to make that all–important transition to the screen.

4. The Same-o, Same-o Syndrome.

In an effort to mimic other popular movies of the day, many writers feel the need to follow a specific story pattern ("formula") too closely. Their reasoning? If it was successful for a particular popular movie, it should work for their projects as well. Unfortunately, the resulting screenplay is usually put in the rejection pile because buyers see it as the "same old" story.

A successful screenwriter once told me: Think of your movie as a cake. Cakes have certain standard ingredients, like flour, eggs, and oil. But some look and taste better than others because their creators deviated from the recipe, adding new ingredients, omitting others, changing the proportions slightly, adopting new techniques, and experimenting with the presentation for an inventive, unique, and hopefully successful end product.

By infusing your script with innovative style, creative plotting, distinctive characters and fresh dialogue, you too can go a long way in avoiding that feeling of "sameness." Do not be afraid to add a few unique twists to your project, or to add some unexpected, satisfying elements that will delight and surprise your audience.

Buyers realize that there are only so many basic storylines that have been utilized since the days of the cavemen, but when a writer submits a project with a protagonist or antagonist that has a unique or intriguing point of view, you can be sure your project and your creative "take" on your character's perspective on life will put your script in the much-coveted 10% pile of "Considers" or "Recommends."

5. The Know-It-All/Sloppy Sam.

Submissions that fall into this particular rejection category include "The Know-It-All" — the writer who has selected an area of expertise and is determined to tell us everything he knows about the subject, the unfortunate result being that the storyline gets loaded down with too many unnecessary details — details like the kind of design on the buttons on a Victorian gentleman's topcoat, or the specific version of a jazz classic playing in the background of a scene. This sort of detail usually results in impeding the pacing of the story, undercutting the escalation of the plot, and taking away from the development of the characters. So, unless those fancy Victorian buttons on the villain's topcoat specifically lead to your character's downfall, or the specific version of that jazz classic is the key to solving your mystery, it really is best to keep such overly researched details to an absolute minimum.

On the other hand, a common pet peeve among potential buyers is what I call "The Sloppy Sam" — a writer whose screenplay is lacking in key details and contains very little in the way of stylish, visual atmospherics or color. The Sloppy Sam has not taken the time to do important research, has given us inaccurate information, and/ or provided his storyline with only vague logic. Simply putting "EXT. MANHATTAN — STREET" is not sufficient enough to make the reader feel that they are in Manhattan, for instance. One or two sentences is all that is needed to give us a more distinct feeling of whether we are in the ritzy Upper East Side of Fifth Avenue or in the dark, gritty recesses and broken-dream alleyways of Alphabet City in Lower Manhattan.

The writer has to keep in mind that the audience has paid good money to be transported to the world where your characters will meet, confront, and be challenged by their demons and fears before fulfilling their dreams two hours later. If the world is unfamiliar (e.g., in another galaxy, in a past era, in the future, in a make-believe country), it is the writer's responsibility to not only establish that unfamiliar world, but to make the audience (and the potential buyer) believe in that world and the marvels and dangers it may hold.

6. Flashback/Voiceover Hell.

While this reason for a rejection is more often symptomatic of the novice writer, from time to time some experienced scripters have confessed that they, too, will become stumped on how to insert information or backstory into their script. In desperation, they will often turn to flashbacks or voice overs to do their storytelling for them. Unfortunately, if not used properly and sparingly, flashbacks and voice overs can end up sinking a movie by confusing an audience and sidetracking them from the main storyline.

As a nostalgic device, voice overs can sometimes be appropriate and effective; remember how a voice over helped to establish the multiple mother-daughter relationships amongst four families in *The Joy Luck Club*? Flashbacks and flash-forwards can also be effective as a stylized storytelling device, as was the case in the fairy tale film *The Princess Bride*, where the movie would cut back to Peter Falk, playing a character who is telling the story to his enthralled grandson.

If faced with the temptation to use a flashback, flash-forward or voice over, you should first consider reviewing your story to see if the information you are trying to relay can be cleverly inserted, perhaps via dialogue, into a meaningful, related conversation. Another reason for the red flag on flashbacks is a financial one. Flashbacks often involve another period of time and can add appreciably to a film's budget in terms of sets, costumes, props, and additional acting talent.

7. The Kitchen Sink Theory.

It has been said that we cannot please all of the people all of the time, yet many scripters still insist on trying to accomplish this goal by putting "everything but the kitchen sink" into a their film project — just to prove that their movie has "something for everyone."

This theory reminds me of a submission that was sent to a studio story department several years ago. The basic premise was: "A young couple falls in love and time travels to outer space." Yet within the 125 pages, the young couple sang their way out of an underwater prison ruled by misplaced inhabitants from Atlantis and had an out-of-body experience where mythical figures warned them that, like history, they were doomed to repeat their mistakes with disastrous results. They *also* found time to flee to a lost galaxy to find happiness, while helping the inhabitants of the galaxy to uncover the secret to survival.

The screenplay's cover letter sincerely and proudly announced to all, "Here is a movie that will appeal to the masses." Sadly, the script's tone fluctuated wildly from outright melodrama to camp humor because the writer attempted to crowd way too many genres into one film: science fiction, fantasy, mythology, drama, comedy, musical, melodrama, mystery, and romance!

Even in the highly imaginative and often improbable world of moviemaking, we cannot expect the audience to take too many leaps of faith at one given time.

8. The Yakkety-Yak Trap.

Executives, agents and producers concur that dialogue is one of the key ingredients in the sale of most screenplays. Yet many writers get carried away, writing long dramatic speeches for their characters, either to drive home a point or to convey a piece of plotting.

Another sign of what is known as "The Yakkety-Yak Trap" is the conversation that drags on much too long. When the page count starts to mount, the wise writer will carefully review his dialogue, vigilantly aware that lengthy discussions and meaningless monologues seldom have a place in a *moving* picture.

Instead of "talking" about their feelings, is there some way that you can "show" your characters in action?

In the first few minutes of *Witness* there are no words, but the subtle play of movement and emotions on the face of the Kelly McGillis character as she struggles with her new widowhood and the care of her young son speaks volumes.

In the romantic comedy *Something's Gotta Give*, there is a funny, but effective, montage in which we see the Diane Keaton character trying to get over her break-up with Jack Nicholson as she purges all of her emotions into writing a play based on their relationship.

Always keep in mind that the most interesting and revealing conversations always come *after* the initial small talk. Though reality has us starting a conversation with "Hi, how are you? How's the family?" and ending with "Goodbye. Take care. I'll see you around," what an audience really needs to hear is what falls in between — the meat of the conversation, with as little fat as possible. As they say in The Biz — "Show, don't tell."

9. The "Wannabe" Screenplay — spec script vs. shooting script.

One of the most common mistakes a new scripter can inadvertently make is to submit their "spec script" in the wrong format. The margins and tabs may be correct, but there are other signs a screenplay is by a non-professional (aka "wannabe") writer.

When writing a screenplay, it is important to know the difference between a "spec script" (also known as a "reading script") and a "shooting script."

What is a "shooting script"?

To become familiar with screenwriting, many writers will look at scripts of successfully produced movies in the same genre as their project to become acquainted with how a professional screenwriter handles structure, character interaction, dialogue, pacing, tension, comedic timing, action sequences, etc. Generally speaking, the screenplays found on the Internet or ordered online are **shooting scripts**, which are the final revised and approved screenplay that a director, cast and crew will use on the set of a production.

Shooting scripts are much more detailed and may include additional elements usually not found in a spec script, such as:

> Scene numbers.

> A large number of camera angles and directions.

> Detailed descriptions of special effects.

> Detailed descriptions of stuntwork/action set pieces.

> Specific information regarding set design, costuming, lighting.

> Special notations (if needed) regarding acting.

Shooting scripts are also usually much longer in page count than a spec or reading script. Once a project goes into production, everyone on the set needs to work off of the same document containing all the directions and specific notations mentioned above, which is why it is called a shooting script. It is interesting to note that even though a project is in production, it is not at all unusual to have revisions made to the shooting script — changes in dialogue, an added or deleted scene, camera angles, etc.

Why can't I include all the details of a "shooting script" in my "spec script"?

Most shooting scripts have gone through several revisions to accommodate the creative needs of the actors, director, set/costume designers, special effects director, and other production personnel. In fact, most shooting scripts can be from ten pages to forty pages longer than a spec/reading script. Reading through the additional details when a project is first submitted can affect the reader's ability to accurately judge such things as pacing, tension, comedic timing, etc.

Equally as important — since making movies is a business — all potential projects are subject to such business concerns as budgeting and marketing.

Agents, producers and executives who are reading new material submitted to them are mostly concerned with the potential of the storyline. Also, if you do not have any produced material, agents and managers may send out your spec/reading scripts as a **writing sample** to a producer or studio that might be looking for a writer to do a rewrite in the same genre as your spec/reading screenplay.

What is a "spec script"?

A **spec script** — whether it is an original story or based on previous material — is a script a writer has written "on speculation" (unpaid) for the following considerations:

> As a possible film/television project for outright purchase/sale or option.

> As a writing sample that serves to introduce a screenwriter so that others may evaluate their overall talent, usually in anticipation of a potential writing assignment for a rewrite or "polish" on another project a studio or production company may already own, or to find a writer to help write and develop an in-house idea.

> As a writing sample that introduces a screenwriter to an agent or manager for possible representation as a new client.

As mentioned above, agents, producers and executives who are always on the prowl for new clients or new projects are mainly focused on the storyline and whether or not it is saleable and can fit into a company's or studio's budgetary range and development slate. Reading a document like a shooting script can often be more confusing because of the extra production details that can inadvertently give the impression that the pacing is too slow. In addition, those extra notes can also undercut the comedic timing and action sequences.

Spec scripts should always be spare and lean because the main purpose of this initial script is to determine if the storyline is compelling and intriguing enough to take you on as a new client, or to offer you an option or purchase of your script.

To that end, screenwriters need to adhere to the following when submitting a spec or reading script:

▸ Descriptive narrative: Remember to give just enough description to set the scene. While detailed descriptions of the colors and formations of the canyons, the desert and the evening sky as your protagonist is furiously galloping through the area may be an integral part of the enjoyment of the reading process in a novel, you will need to stick to a more concise narrative in a script.

EXAMPLE:

EXT. DESERT CANYON – SUNSET

A Gunman races through the rocky canyon, his horse leaving a cloud of dust in its wake.

▸ Descriptive character action: There is no need to worry about putting down every movement or facial expression your characters makes (e.g., having your heroine take off her tattered coat, put it on a hanger, hang it in a closet, have her turn around, go to the hot plate to make tea, pour it into her cup, then take a seat in her favorite chair by the window, have her heave a sigh as she sips her tea and begins petting her black cat). Again, stick to the basics of the scene:

EXAMPLE:

INT. BEV'S STUDIO APARTMENT – EARLY EVENING

Another difficult day behind her, Bev settles down with her cup of tea, her faithful black cat on her lap.

▸ Descriptive action sequences: Keep your action scenes to a minimum. No need to describe each and every thrust and parry as the two knights are battling one another — give just enough description so we have a sense of what the action is all about. A major complaint from producers and executives is when the action sequences are so heavily detailed, and oftentimes so awkwardly written, that it becomes difficult to understand at first read. This means these scenes have to be re-read in order to better understand what a writer may be trying to convey. Even after re-reading them, there still may be some residual confusion. Writers are advised to try and keep it simple and allow the stunt coordinator and director to confer on the exact choreographic details.

EXAMPLE:
EXT. ROCKY SCOTTISH HIGHLANDS – DAY
The White Knight plows through the melee until he reaches his target — The Black Knight. There is instant recognition as their eyes meet. In a violent flurry of slashing blades, the Black Knight suffers a bloody, fatal blow and the White Knight is left standing, battered, but victorious.

▶ Camera angles: Eliminate most of the camera angles. It is all right to use an occasional "cut to" or "fade in" or "close up" if you feel it is necessary. Just keep in mind that eventually a director will read your script and he will undoubtedly have his own vision for how each scene should be shot.

▶ Sounds: If sounds play an important part in your scene, you should definitely put the sound in CAPS for more emphasis. Sounds really can add another layer or dimension to a scene, enhancing the dramatic tension of a thriller or emphasizing the humor in a comedy. In other words, the reader is not simply just looking at words on the page, but will actually think about and possibly "hear" sounds when he sees a sound in CAPS. This is all part of giving the reader a heightened feeling of actually experiencing your screenplay as a motion picture, which is one of the main goals you want to achieve when someone reads the script you have submitted.

EXAMPLE:
INT. DARKENED CELLAR – DAY
Blindfolded, bound and gagged, Charlotte comes to, unsure of where she is. Suddenly she hears the unmistakable TICKING of a clock… is it a timing device wired to an explosive? She hears VOICES downstairs and begins furiously STOMPING her feet against the wooden floor, hoping someone — anyone — will find her before the timer runs out.

> ▸ Introducing Characters: When a character with a speaking role makes their first appearance in the screenplay, remember to put the character's names in CAPS. This will alert the reader to a new role. There is no need to continue to put the character's name in caps thereafter.

EXAMPLE:
EXT. GARDEN ENTRANCE – AFTERNOON
The gate is ajar. A hand pushes it open and a slender young girl, LORI, enters the garden. Her eyes light up as a small, playful black and tan dog runs up to greet her. Lori picks up the dog as it licks her face in joyful recognition.

> ▸ Scene Numbers: Even if you are a writer-director, do not submit a reading script with scene numbers. As mentioned previously, most screenplays go through a series of revisions as the project is developed and fine-tuned. When a producer or studio exec opens up a submitted screenplay and spots numbered scenes, they automatically will assume that the material is from a novice writer.

> ▸ Formatting: Except for what is mentioned above, the format for a spec or reading script is essentially the same as it is for a shooting script.

Hopefully by using this chapter as a guideline, your screenplay will have a better chance of sitting atop that coveted "Consider" or "Recommend" pile!

Chapter 9

Walkin' The Walk:
Creating Opportunities For Yourself

A dozen Hollywood agents received a personally addressed fax
with the following message: "Per our conversation, I'm sending by
courier the hot spec from the new writer we discussed. Let me know
what you think." The fax was signed with an indecipherable scrawl.
A script with the same message arrived at each agent's office later
that day. The only way to contact the mysterious sender was to call
the phone number on the last page of the script, which belonged to
a very gutsy new screenwriter. Although most of the agents didn't
appreciate being duped, one admitted he liked the scripter's high-
concept thriller enough that he agreed to send it to half a dozen of
his producing clients. If one of them wanted to take on the project
the agent would gladly represent the writer. None of the producers
liked the script enough to make it one of their projects, but at least
the writer got twelve top agents and six well-known producers to
read his work!

SUNDANCE SCREENWRITING LAB NEARING DEADLINE

TOP SCRIPTERS FETED AT MOONDANCE FILM FESTIVAL

FOUR WIN NICHOLL FELLOWSHIPS

UCLA COMEDY COMPETITION AWARDS ANNOUNCED

CBS ANNOUNCES DIVERSITY WRITING WINNERS

The above are just a few of the headlines that have merited feature articles in the Hollywood trade papers throughout the past year. These headlines are yet another reminder to us of an alternate way in which a new or emerging scriptwriter can break into The Biz and get his work noticed by the industry. Screenwriting competitions and fellowships are an excellent way to announce to the world that you have got "the write stuff." And with the Internet, writers have found a new tool in which to gain recognition and to market their work.

Let's start with the screenwriting contests and fellowships first. What is the difference between a scriptwriting competition and a fellowship program? Which contests are best to enter and why?

Fellowships.

Fellowships are usually scholarships that will enable new screenwriters to practice and polish their craft under the experienced and watchful tutelage of professionals in the entertainment industry. Some of the fellowships are for as short as three months, while others can be for as long as a year. Usually a specified amount of money is given to each "fellow" (recipient) which will provide either full or partial support while the writer is learning the tricks of the trade as he sharpens his craft. During their tenure as fellows, writers will work under the careful guidance and supervision of a development or creative group at a studio or with a producer and his staff of writers on a television series.

Some fellowships are specific — usually for either television or features. If they are for television, some fellowships are divided up into drama or comedy development. Most fellowship entries are read by a

118

team of creative executives and story analysts who work for the studio or production company sponsoring the program. In addition to having his work evaluated on an industry level, the writer will have his style, his attention to character development and dialogue, and his professional work ethics assessed.

Once the fellowship entrants are narrowed down to a more elite pool, telephone calls are placed to the semifinalists. Each is given the news of his lucky status and is asked a variety of questions — first and foremost: If chosen, will the writer be able to drop what he is doing and move to the Los Angeles area for the duration of the fellowship training? Other questions are designed to determine the potential recipient's experience level as a writer as well as his ability to adjust to such industry expectations as long hours, flexible schedules, and working with a variety of egos and personalities.

After the semifinalists have been interviewed, members of the creative group narrow the list to the writers who they feel are not only the most talented, but possess the determination, drive and adaptability to make the most out of the fellowship program.

During their tenure, fellowship recipients will work on both their own projects and on a variety of in-house assignments as well. For a television fellowship, a writer may be assigned to a specific show to work with a staff of writers. If the fellowship is for motion pictures, the writer will usually be paired with at least one or two members of the film division's creative group (ideally a senior vice president and a director of development) where he will come up with potential ideas for new projects while receiving feedback on the development of his own projects.

In some instances, if a fellow and their contribution to the creative group are well received, they may be given an opportunity to continue their fellowship for an additional six months or a year. And in some cases where the fellowship is for television, a successful recipient may end up being given an opportunity to write one or two episodes for a coming season.

Competitions and contests.

Competitions can vary in considerably different ways. Some offer no more than a nice piece of paper declaring the winner of the contest, while others may offer cash prizes, scriptwriting-related prizes (subscriptions to trade papers, free postings on marketing websites, screenwriting software, etc.), and other opportunities. Most of these contests are sponsored by writing organizations, universities, film commissions, film festivals or production companies.

The persons judging these competitions can vary from local volunteers or interns to organization members and professionals in the entertainment industry. While it is quite common for local volunteers or organization members to judge the preliminary round of a contest, the best competitions to enter are those in which the final judges serve a professional capacity in either film or television — studio executives, producers, agents, script consultants entertainment attorneys, development specialists, or screenwriters.

In competitions where there are several hundred or a few thousand entries, there are at least three or four rounds of judging and these multiple rounds can take several months. Writers who progress to the quarterfinals and semifinals are usually notified by mail or email of their status (not necessarily the case in smaller contests). When the judging is down to the finalists, those writers are notified of the date, time and location where the winners will be revealed and introduced. In most cases, it is up to the finalist to pay for their own transportation and lodging to these events. One of the possible key benefits of attending these events is the opportunity to network with the final judges.

Fees.

Take note. Most contests and fellowships usually require some sort of an entry fee — generally used to help defray the cost of such expenses as mailing, logging in material, copying, paying for visiting judges, and other administrative costs incurred in running such a contest. Fees can range anywhere from $25 up to $100+, although most seem to hover closer to the $50 range.

Some contests, in an effort to avoid a last-day flood of entries, have utilized a multi-tiered fee system, whereby the earlier you submit your script, the less you pay. Note that no matter what the entry fee, some competitions have what is called an "entry cap," or limit on the number of entries they will allow to be entered into competition.

Why should I enter?

Entering fellowships and/or competitions offers several benefits to the unproduced screenwriter:

> First, this is an excellent way to test the water and find out how others, especially those in the industry, will respond to your story and to your writing talent.

> Second, it can be a significant and ego-boosting way to gain recognition for your writing efforts. Every writer deserves to have his or her work validated.

> Third, depending on how prestigious the fellowship or contest may be, your script may be read by agents, producers or studio execs who are eager to find new clients, new projects, and new candidates for rewrites and in-house projects.

How do I enter?

Here are some "common sense" guidelines:

> Complete and polish your script. If you belong to a writing group, have a few members of your group read and proof your screenplay for professional appearance, content and writing style. If you desire, you may want to get a professional critique to help you with a rewrite.

> Read the trade papers (*The Hollywood Reporter* and *Variety*, for example). Publications like *Writer's Digest* and *Creative Screenwriting* also feature news about scriptwriting contests, and the online newsletter *The Hollywood Scriptwriter* routinely contains articles on upcoming fellowships, film festivals, and competitions. You

may also want to check other websites and chat rooms devoted to screenwriting to find out what your fellow scripters know about upcoming contests.

> Make a list of the competitions and fellowships that most interest you. Carefully note their fees and deadlines. Unless you thrive on stress, it is advisable not to submit your material at the very last minute. Be sure and allow yourself plenty of time to realistically mull over and revise your work once it is nearly completed. New writers often have that uncontrollable urge to send their material out the minute they have typed in the last "FADE OUT." Suppress that urge. Seasoned writers will tell you that writing "The End" is only the very beginning.

> Look over all rules and guidelines very carefully. Some contests and fellowships specify what they will or will not accept. For example, some contests are very specific and will accept only family-oriented scripts or faith-based stories or will accept only screenplays in which a majority of the movie can be filmed in a particular state or location. Most competitions are for unproduced writers (those whose work has not been turned into a theatrical or television film). A few competitions will accept scripts that have been optioned but not yet produced. Of special note for those who qualify are those fellowships or competitions that focus on encouraging minorities (women, writers of color, writers over forty, etc.). You may want to send a query letter if the guidelines are not clear to you. If there is a phone number or a website address, do not hesitate to contact the sponsoring company or organization for answers to your questions.

> Follow all instructions to the letter. If the competition asks for the first fifteen pages of your script and a two-page, double-spaced synopsis of the rest of your story, do not submit the first eighteen pages and a three-page, single-spaced synopsis. If the contest limits you to one script, not to exceed 125 pages, do not send your 138-page screenplay. If the directions ask that you put only the title on the front page, do not be tempted to add your

name. (Most competitions are deliberately judged "blind" so that those reading the material will not be tempted to give preference to a writer they might know.) If a self-addressed stamped envelope (SASE) is requested, remember to include an envelope large enough and with enough postage to allow for the return of your material. In most cases, the sponsoring organization will not return any screenplays. Fill out your entry form by printing all requested information legibly and completely.

One administrator for a well-known fellowship competition told me that she has had to routinely disqualify as much as 15% of the entries in the annual screenwriting program she oversees, simply because writers neglected to read and follow the directions carefully. Make sure you do not waste such a significant investment of time, talent and money, only to be disqualified for not following the instructions and rules.

Which competitions should I enter?

No matter how large or how small, all competitions have some importance and serve a common purpose: to recognize and herald the accomplishments of writers. Some writers prefer to start out by entering smaller, local contests where they can hopefully gain a bit more confidence before branching out into larger, international competitions. If you are interested specifically in a fellowship program but live outside the Los Angeles area, you will have to seriously weigh the possibility of moving to and living in the Los Angeles area for an extended period of time.

Being a finalist can bring instant recognition, especially if the judges are professionals in the entertainment industry and include agents, producers or studio executives. Carefully check competition brochures and websites for an indication of how the final judging will be conducted. And do not be afraid to inquire if industry professionals will be part of the final judging process. Although the sponsors may not be able to tell you exactly who will be part of the final judging panel, you may want to ask for the names of past judges, or at least for the names of the studios, production companies or agencies for which they have worked. The answer should give you an excellent idea of the professional caliber that is associated with the contest.

The Big Wait.

Keep in mind that the number of script submissions for these competitions is usually quite high. The Nicholl Fellowship alone receives in excess of 3,500 entries every year, from all corners of the world. Reaching the semifinals or finals of the Nicholl competition is considered quite a coup, given the large number of entrants annually. The Walt Disney Company Screenwriting Fellowship Program receives more than 1,200 submissions every year.

You should expect to wait anywhere from one to six months after the entry deadline before winners are announced. If you have not heard from the sponsoring organization after a reasonable period of time, or if they do not have a specific date noted on their brochure or website to announce their winners, you may want to send a SASE requesting a list.

During the long wait, continue to work on your next television or motion picture project. You should also look ahead toward entering other competitions or applying for fellowships. While being a finalist or even a winner does not guarantee a lucrative writing career, it can be an all-important "door opener" toward obtaining an agent for your work or securing that coveted and rare opportunity to submit your material to a producer.

Making the most if you are a finalist.

After the winners have been announced, most studios and production entities will assign at least one or two development or creative executives to read and evaluate the final submissions of most of the major competitions. This is also standard operating procedure with most of Hollywood's larger literary agencies, which will have a team of junior agents evaluate the work of the finalists.

If you are a finalist, consider contacting various agencies and production companies by mail. In the letter, mention your recent accomplishment, stating the genre, along with a two-sentence log line or elevator pitch on your script. It is not unheard of for many of the finalists of the major competitions to obtain agency representation and/or an option offer from a production company — even if they do not receive the top prize.

To help get you started, here are some screenwriting fellowships and script competitions recommended by industry colleagues and many of my writing clients. In addition, check your local and state film commissions and film festivals to see if they are holding a screenwriting contest.

- ▸ Final Draft Big Break Competition
- ▸ Scriptapalooza International Competition
- ▸ Scriptapalooza TV Competition
- ▸ Script P.I.M.P. Screenwriting Competition
- ▸ Script P.I.M.P. Television Competition
- ▸ Page International Screenwriting Awards
- ▸ Acclaim Scripts Film & Television Script Writing Contests
- ▸ Creative Screenwriting Magazine AAA Screenplay Contest
- ▸ Hollywood Outreach Program
- ▸ Carl Sautter Memorial Outreach Program
- ▸ The Nicholl Fellowship
- ▸ Austin Film Festival Screenplay and Teleplay Competitions
- ▸ Zoetrope Screenplay Contest
- ▸ NBC Writers On The Verge
- ▸ NBC Diversity Initiative for Writers
- ▸ CBS Diversity Institute: Writers Mentoring Program
- ▸ ABC/Disney Television Writing Fellowship
- ▸ Warner Bros. Writers Workshop
- ▸ Fox Writer's Initiative
- ▸ Nickelodeon Writing Fellowship Program

Chapter 10

Stayin' Alive:
Resolutions To Keep You Productive
And Challenged As A Writer

In the faraway kingdom of Arkansas, a writer who was recently divorced and unemployed agreed to work as a house-/dog-sitter for his dentist while she was on a summer-long trip to Europe. The writer figured this would serve as a self-imposed "retreat" so he could polish his script and start on his next project. Halfway through the summer, however, he gets a call from his dentist — her sister needs a vacation and is going to be staying at the house. The sister arrives and the writer returns to his cross-town apartment. A few days later, the sister visits with the dog in tow — it seems the writer left a draft of his script at the house. Embarrassed, the writer apologizes and the dentist's sister tells him he shouldn't apologize — she liked his script and thinks he has talent. He asks her how she would know, and she replies, "Because I'm an agent and I'd like to represent you."

Who knew that housesitting or dog walking could end up being so productive? Just shows you never know when you might get your big break!

One of the most common laments among writers is "What do I do while waiting for my script to sell?" Aside from encouraging you to continue to work on your next project, keeping yourself productive and motivated at any stage of the writing game can be your biggest challenge. Here are some resolutions to keep you going, no matter if you are waiting for the big sale or just getting started in "the game."

Write every day.

Easier said than done, but a true writer really does write just about every single day. Set a goal for yourself. Make it a "do-able" goal, be it one scene a day, Act One of your selling synopsis, polishing your query letter, a detailed character breakdown, or the opening paragraph for setting the scene of your new screenplay.

When you do not feel motivated to work on your current project, brainstorm new ideas or write in your diary or journal. If you are traveling, describe in a paragraph the sights, sounds and smells of the day.

Keep a pad (or notebook) and pencil handy — on your night-stand to record memorable dreams, by the phone and in your car to capture ideas that spring up while you listen to talkative relatives or wait in traffic.

Some writers are never without their hand-held organizers, netbooks or iPads to record great notions for future projects or solutions to current ones. Inspirations, like opportunities, often come to us at the most unexpected moments — so be prepared to capture them.

Start a marketing list.

Find and pursue at least one or two marketing possibilities each week. Even successful writers who have an agent, entertainment attorney or manager create opportunities for themselves. If you do not subscribe to one of the trade papers, try your local library for copies, or go in with another fellow scripter for a subscription. Both *Variety* and *The Hollywood Reporter* occasionally offer free 30-day trial subscriptions.

Do not forget to scour the weekend entertainment sections of the larger metropolitan papers; they contain fodder for marketing prospects. Gossip columns, which often mention the name of a star's new production company, and radio and television segments that focus on entertainment are also potential goldmines of current information, along with such magazines as *People* and *US Weekly*.

Other marketing sources include the fore-mentioned *The Hollywood Creative Directory* and *The Hollywood Representation Directory*, as well as *The Hollywood Distributor's Directory*. Online sources include Movie-Bytes (*moviebytes.com*), The Internet Movie Database (*imdb.com*), Done Deal Pro (*donedealpro.com*), InkTip (*inktip.com*), and Hollywood Lit Sales (*hollywoodlitsales.com*). For those screenwriters in Europe, check out TwelvePoint (*twelvepoint.com*) for additional information and resources.

Make notes or clip items and, if you are trying to market or sell your project, act upon them. If you are not quite at this point, file the items for further action in a separate marketing file (multi-compartment accordion files work well) until you are ready to make your move.

Network.

The most productive place to network is at a writing conference, film festival or pitchfest. Here you will have opportunities to meet agents, producers, studio executives, writers, and other undiscovered scripters like yourself.

The importance of developing good networking skills cannot be stressed enough. Gathering and sharing information is a key component in succeeding and maintaining a career in the entertainment industry. The art of networking is so vital (the entire next chapter is devoted to the subject).

If there is a local screenwriting group, consider joining. If there is not a group, think about starting one of your own or join an organization like Scriptwriters Network (*scriptwritersnetwork.org*), which is based in the Los Angeles area, but has members all over North America. If you live in Washington or Oregon, consider joining the Northwest Screenwriters Guild (*nwsg.org*). If you reside in or around the Wisconsin area, contact the Wisconsin Screenwriters Forum (*wiscreenwritersforum.org*). Another possibility is to join the Writer's Store group, StoryLink (*storylink.com/group/screenwriting*), which has members worldwide. All of these groups share information and often critique one another's scripts, while providing valuable advice and information on their website.

Become a volunteer at a nearby film festival or call your local film commission. Ask if you can volunteer at any events or spend a couple of hours each week as an intern there, or at a local television station or video production house. State film commissions will often sponsor a screenwriting competition, but if you are not yet ready to enter the competition yourself, but would like to participate and gain a little insight into the screenwriting process, consider being a volunteer for the preliminary judging.

You may want to consider volunteering at one of the screen-writing conferences or pitchfests. These volunteer positions are much coveted, but have proven to be quite beneficial from a networking and informational standpoint. Volunteer responsibilities range from checking in V.I.P. speakers/faculty, monitoring one-on-one appointments, introducing speakers at their workshop, or being a speaker's "assistant" for a day. One fortunate volunteer at a writing conference drove an agent to the airport, only to learn her plane was delayed. The volunteer decided to stay with the agent until her departure. During that time the agent found out the volunteer had written a proposal for an animated children's tale. Turns out a producing client for one of her colleagues at the agency was looking for an animated project for a younger audience. She asked the volunteer to email the proposal to her and promised she would give it to her colleague.

If a nearby college or university has a screenwriting course, think about taking the course, not only to gain additional knowledge and information, but also to network with other course participants who might become valuable allies and supporters. These classes are also an ideal venue to find writers interested in joining a writing group.

Other writers have found that taking a couple of acting classes and volunteering at local theater groups (even if it is doing work behind-the-scenes) have helped them to create stronger characters and write better dialogue, as well as giving them a more complete understanding of just how vital a screenplay actually is — the all-important blueprint that each actor, director and member of the crew must follow if the play, episode or movie is going to have a fighting chance to be accepted by the public.

If your 9-to-5 job or family commitments prevent you from going outside the home, you might want to consider brushing up in areas like dialogue, structure, pitching, writing treatments and characterization by taking online classes. Three sources where screenwriters can get such instruction include Writers University (*writersuniverity.com*), Media Bistro (*mediabistro.com*), and Gotham Writers Workshop (*writingclasses.com*).

If your local newspaper does not have a film critic and if you are an avid movie buff, take a leap of faith and call the paper and ask if they might be interested in hiring you. Of course, it is advisable to have a few sample critiques to demonstrate your writing style. If your local paper already has a film critic, they may be flattered if you ask if you can pick their brain about screenwriting.

All of the above are potential gardens of information to cultivate and harvest.

See more movies.

At the risk of sounding silly, when I advise seeing movies, I mean all kinds of movies. With the wide range of DVDs available and with so many movie channels on cable, there is no reason not to view at least one or two films a week. And while you may want to concentrate on great romantic classics because that is the genre of your current project, you should also broaden your perspective.

Seeing all kinds of motion pictures means keeping an open mind and expanding your moviegoing knowledge by viewing "bad" movies and different genres, even those you do not particularly like. Writers can get a better understanding of what works and what does not by watching films that are totally unfamiliar.

There is an art to watching films:

> If you are at a theater, sit as close to the middle of the theater as possible. Never sit in the first front five rows (unless you are

hard of hearing, have forgotten your glasses, or are in one of those tiny multiplex theaters with only ten rows). I usually sit at least twelve rows from the front and five rows from the back because this allows me the most viewing pleasure and gives me a greater arena for audience observation.

> Before the lights dim, look around. What is the age range of the audience? Which age group makes up the greater percentage of those present? Is this audience composed mostly of males or females? What's the cultural, racial and socio-economic make-up of the people there? This kind of information helps writers pinpoint the demographic appeal of a movie, which is one of the key elements used when a production company or studio decides to purchase a script. Some films appeal to a broader audience than others. Surprisingly, there are some movies that, on the surface, seem to appeal to a narrower segment of mov-iegoers but end up crossing over and appealing to the general public. Some examples include *Little Miss Sunshine, My Big Fat Greek Wedding, Juno,* and *The Full Monty.*

> As you watch the film, ask: What is this movie about? What is the main goal of the protagonist? Who or what serves as the protagonist's main challenge or opposition and why? Has anyone walked out yet? The first thirty minutes or so should provide the setup of the story and coincides with the first thirty to thirty-five pages of a script.

> By the end of the first hour, it is time to ask: Is the protagonist's plan of action in place? Have there been enough complications and plot twists to keep the audience interested? Or are there so many subplots and story points that the film is becoming too plot-heavy? Conversely, is the story so simple and uneventful that the audience is quickly losing interest? This is the all-important midsection of the story, where many a film (or script) can fall apart.

> Toward the end of the movie, you should notice if the audience is fully behind the protagonist's attempts for success. Can you

sense that people are rooting for the protagonist? In the more successful action films, the audience will sometimes talk back to the screen as they cheer the hero on to victory.

> Throughout the film, observe the following: Which scenes get the best response? Which scenes fall flat? What character(s) get the best and the worst responses from the audience? Which lines make the audience emotionally react?

> As the audience files out, what are some of the comments you overhear? Does the audience stay for the credits (usually a good sign that they didn't want this movie experience to end)? Try to stay seated through the credits whenever possible. They contain valuable information, such as where the film was shot, who provided those wonderful sets, what design house created those innovative titles, who the actor was whose two lines stole the scene in the first act, or what production company made the film. You never know when this information will prove useful.

> Once home, analyze the audience reaction using the following questions: Was the movie too long? Was it too short? Were there signs of restlessness from the audience and, if so, in which section of the story? Did you notice people constantly checking their watches? Did anyone walk out of the film? Why did the movie succeed or fail from the viewpoint of the story? Why did the movie succeed or fail in any other aspects, like direction, acting, etc.?

> Assess the "look" of the film by considering the locations, special effects, stunts, setting, and how much impact each of these elements played upon the overall movie. When evaluating scripts, story analysts will always consider whether the story justifies the cost of production. Obviously, the more commercial potential a film has, the more money the studio or production company will be willing to spend on such high-ticketed items as locations, effects, etc. It is also interesting to notice, when a film is set in a foreign locale or during a different historical period, whether most of the story took place indoors (interiors, which

can be shot on studio sets) or outdoors (exteriors, which require filming on location)?

> Assess other aspects of the film. Was there too much internal, thought-driven story (a difficult thing to communicate realistically on screen) and not enough external action, or vice versa? Were there scenes that required large numbers of extras? Did the stuntwork outshine the story? Consider the impact of such items as the musical score, costume design, and other production values, asking yourself if the final result lived up to the film's production values — that is, the amount spent on production? Remember that people want to value what they see and experience. Will they feel that this film was worth the price of admission?

> Was this a high- or low/soft-concept film? In other words, was this a commercial film with an easy-to-understand focus and appeal (high concept) or was it a more specialized, smaller film (low or soft concept) that might not appeal to a broader audience? Was the movie more plot-driven or character-driven? Or was this that rare film that ably and successfully combined both plot and characterization (*A Beautiful Mind, The Shawshank Redemption,* and *Slumdog Millionaire* are good examples of this winning combination).

> What was the marketing focus of the film? Did you see trailers for this movie? If so, did they successfully encourage you to see the film? Do you remember the trailers? What did they show? Look at the film's theater posters (one-sheets) and its newspaper and magazine ads for clues to how the audience was wooed. In many cases, moviegoers comment that the coming attraction for a film was far better than the actual film.

> Assess your gut reaction. Were you entertained by this movie? Would you recommend this film to your friends or family? If not, why not? How could this film be improved from the viewpoint of story? Was there any part of the story that confused you? Did you understand each character's purpose and reason

for being included in the story? Was the dialogue effective in helping to mold the growth and personalities of the characters while moving the story forward?

Get into people-watching.

Writers have often mentioned that some of the best stories and characters come from simply observing life around them. Some of their favorite places to people-watch are crowded areas like airports, college campuses, parks, shopping malls, train or subway stations, amusement parks, parties and restaurants. One writer tells me that some of his most colorful and interesting characters for his stories were "born" in Las Vegas — that is, he observed people who piqued his imagination and made him wonder: Who are they? Why are they in Las Vegas? Do they really want to be there? What do they do for a living? Do they have a family? What are they feeling at the moment? Notice how they are dressed, along with their posture, their attitude. Are they self-assured and confident or the exact opposite? Do they have any unusual physical traits or mannerisms? Do they have any annoying habits or unique quirks? And most of all, what do you think their backstory is up to this point in their life?

Everyone has a history, and it is fun to build a personality and story around a person who catches your eye. One helpful hint: Do not be too obvious in your people-watching or your creative efforts might be misconstrued!

Read, read, read.

In addition to your daily local newspaper (an absolute must) and the entertainment section online, scan as many current affairs and specialty publications as you can. *Variety, People, US Weekly,* and *The Hollywood Reporter* have already been mentioned, but consider looking at such publications as *Time, The American Medical Journal, Scientific Monthly, The Wall Street Journal, Readers Digest,* and *Newsweek.* Read, not just for the entertainment segments of the magazine or newspaper, but for that unexpected piece of information you might need for your project. Read to glean ideas and to provide background — maybe that article on battered women holds insights for the central character in your latest screenplay, or perhaps the new experimental drug could be the focus of your latest crime thriller.

When reading the trade papers, do not be tempted to only read the film and television reviews. The articles are full of information that can be valuable to you. As for the reviews, read beyond the first paragraph; see what you can learn from the particulars of the review: the critique of the storyline, plotting, characterization, and dialogue.

It is also important to read the reviews in various major magazines and newspapers and on Internet sites. All help to give you a wider perspective of what fare is in the theaters and how particular movies are perceived across the country. Note that the companies that distribute the films will often lift quotations from critics' reviews to help bolster a film's advertisements in newspapers, on billboards and in television commercials. The quotes that writers should look for are those directly related to the screenplay, like "well-crafted story and characters" or "a spine-tingling thriller that will keep you guessing."

On a secondary level, note comments that reflect a critic's reasons for liking or disliking a film. For example, "Despite an intriguing story, the actor can't seem to breathe much life into his role," or "Lush photography, coupled with brilliant costuming, adds to the visual appeal of this fascinating period piece."

As a matter of habit, most writers usually scan the weekly charts of the trade papers that feature the box office standings for the preceding week. These charts provide useful information about what kinds of films are popular, both initially and for the long run. When you read the charts, note the top ten films and pay particular attention to how many weeks each movie has been in release. If a film has been out longer than two weeks, compare its present ranking to the week before. Notice how many screens (theaters) carried the film. Higher concept, bigger-budgeted films like *Iron Man* or *Clash of the Titans* are seen on more than 2,500 screens, while smaller, more character-driven specialty films like *An Education, The Visitor,* or *A Serious Man* may be shown in much fewer theaters. An important number to note is the "per screen average" for each film, for that statistic really indicates how a movie is doing — no matter how wide or how limited its release.

Consider the genre of each movie to determine what the public is going to see, but take heart that in two years that genre may not be enjoying quite as much popularity.

The trade papers carry similar charts for international box office statistics. Note the popular genres and trends in the global marketplace since a great deal of revenue comes from overseas sales. There are also charts for top video and DVD rentals and sales, which comprise a large amount of potential revenue for a feature film. The trades also include ratings charts for network TV offerings and syndicated TV shows.

Read the trades to keep up on the changes at studios, agencies and production companies. Changes to look for include the promotion/ ousting of key individuals whose jobs are to look at or buy screenplays — people such as vice presidents of production, directors of development, and executive story editors, etc. A frequent expression used when a production head steps down is that he is "going indie prod," which means his attorney negotiated a deal allowing the ousted exec to become an independent producer (which could also mean a possible new venue to target for your next project).

Other changes to note in the trades might include a shift in the number of films being produced. Recently, a major studio announced plans to accelerate its feature film slate from twenty films to twenty-five a year. This acceleration was due to the studio's acquisition by a larger, financially healthy new parent company. Acquisition also brings up another area of concern for writers — a change of ownership at a studio, large production company, or agency. Although these changes do not occur every day, they do seem to occur more frequently in years past. Whenever a change in ownership occurs, it is sometimes best to wait until the new regime settles in before submitting material. With new ownership comes the distinct possibility of a change of production executives, with new decision-makers or a shift of agents from one department or agency to another. It can also mean a shift in the type of films being produced.

Look for articles about the purchase of screenplays. A recent article read, Studio X "nabbed the edgy sci-fi script for $500,000 against $800,000." The article further noted, "This move illustrates the company's desire to diversify into producing more adult-focused projects as well as family fare." As you can see, the article gave the dollar amount spent, the genre of the script, as well as the added information that the studio was willing to take a chance on a more adult-focused project. Pay attention to any other information about screenplay sales — the key agents/agency involved, as well as any attachments (producer, director, actor). Sometimes the article will even give a *TV Guide*-type blurb on the script's premise.

The trade papers also have a weekly feature on films in development that states the genre of the film, the production company or the studio, as well as the appropriate address and phone numbers. Sometimes key personnel are also listed, giving you more names to put in your marketing file. If you are torn between writing a thriller or a romantic comedy, it may help to look at the films in development. If there seems to be an overabundance of thrillers, you might want to start on your romantic comedy idea first.

As mentioned earlier, valuable information can be found in gossip columns, entertainment blogs and websites like TMZ. One column recently mentioned that a well-known action director credited his producer wife with finding his next project — a high-tech thriller script. If you have a dynamite action screenplay, it might be worth the time to find out the name of the wife's production company and target her on your "A" list of producers. Chances are in your favor that if she wants to produce your project, she may be able to get her "hot" director husband to lens your movie.

In addition to the trades, newspapers and magazines, consider reading screenplays of produced film and television shows. While watching the finished product may be a lot more entertaining, reading the actual script can be very helpful for writers. The movie you just saw would not have made it onto the big screen unless the script sold. Reading the script can give you an idea of how the writer "hooked" the producer or studio exec into making the commitment to producing the project.

If you are having trouble writing a romantic scene, take a look at a successful film like *The Notebook* to see how the writer handled the emotional tone and physical action that made the movie one of the most popular five-hanky films ever. If you want to set the scene for a futuristic world, why not read the screenplay for *Avatar*? And if you want to attract the same audience as *The Hangover* but wonder how to handle the comedy for individual characters, get a copy of the script.

There are several websites that offer free scripts for download. Among them are SimplyScripts (*simplyscripts.com*), HotScripts (*hotscripts. com*), and Drew's Script-O-Rama (*script-o-rama.com*).

Also, Script City (*scriptcity.com*) is a long-standing resource for all kinds of scripts and teleplays. There is a nominal fee, but their online catalogue is quite extensive and often contains different screenplay versions of the same film, making it easier to determine if you are looking at a shooting script or an earlier version that is closer to the original spec that the writer submitted.

Ask questions.

Questions should be part of your networking skills. When you make a new acquaintance, ask about their work. Ask about their travels, family and interests. You would be surprised how easy it is to find someone who knows someone else who is knowledgeable and willing to discuss an area of expertise. Most people are flattered when a writer asks for an expert opinion, especially when they know what they say might be used in a script.

When friends and acquaintances cannot pave the way to an appropriate expert, experienced writers often "let their fingers do the walking" and make cold calls to the local American Cancer Society, the neighborhood branch of the public library, or the community relations officer of the city police department. And if you are writing in the middle of the night and cannot call anyone for information, the Internet is an excellent and inexpensive source to find out basic information on just about any disease, organization, country, language, culture, crime or subject you can possibly imagine.

Strive to be professional.

One observation about many emerging screenwriters is that they do not always present themselves in a professional way. As a writer, you will always have some area you can work on to achieve a more polished, professional presence. Perhaps you need to develop better phone skills or are having problems with writing your query letters. Maybe it is time to take a seminar on sales techniques to gain more insight on how to sell yourself and your work without going overboard.

One working writer told me that the best workshop she took was one on marketing. She learned how to ask questions that would encourage others to be more open about sharing information. She learned which questions would elicit more than a "Yes" or "No." And after taking the marketing class, she was more observant about doing the proper research, whether it was on the location of her new project, creating a new character, or narrowing down the list of production companies that would be best to approach regarding her just-finished script.

While many writers are not used to speaking up, it is important to be open and ready to express yourself clearly, especially with people who can assist you in making a difference in your career. Another successful writer-producer claims that one of the best investments she ever made was taking an improvisational class at a local comedy club. More on the shy side, she realized she needed to take her own leap of faith if she was going to properly present herself and her projects in a professional manner. She credits that "improv" class with providing her with a better sense of comedic timing in her dialogue, as well as the confidence she needed to get through all the pitchfest appoint-ments, meetings and interviews she had to go through when she was trying to break into Tinseltown.

Being professional also means not taking rejection personally. It means being open to suggestions and criticisms as long as they are constructive. It means taking pride in yourself, but knowing when not to let your pride stand in the way of conducting yourself professionally.

Chapter 11

Navigating Your Way Through The Industry Maze

(aka "Baby, We're So Not In Kansas Anymore!")

When I was an exec at Disney, my assistant buzzed me on the intercom. Someone named David was on the phone, insisting he had met me recently. Thinking that it might have been a person I had spoken to at an industry party, I took the call. David turned out to be a "writer" with a script he wanted to submit. When I asked him where we had met, he hemmed and hawed before finally confessing he had sold me a pair of shoes a few days ago. I asked him how he got my number and he reminded me that he had asked for my place of employment, as was the store's policy whenever a purchase was made by check. He finally admitted it was not store policy, but he had spotted a couple of scripts in my tote bag and wanted to find out where I worked, hopeful that selling me a pair of shoes was all the networking he needed to do to get his big break.

WRONG!

One of the toughest tasks for a writer is the art of networking. Let's face it, writers are used to being locked in a dark, dingy room, far away from the normal light-filled world, alone with no one else but their faithful dog and the sickly glare from a computer screen. It is not part of a writer's natural instinct to seek out and share information or ask for favors from the outside world.

Unfortunately, more than any other kind of writer, a screenwriter will find his career path can fail if the art of networking is not among his arsenal of talents. The rise of anyone participating in The Biz is usually in direct proportion to who they know and what they know and what they do with those contacts and knowledge.

What is "networking"?

In short, networking is the fine art of meeting, greeting and assimilating with others who usually share a common interest — in this case, writing for the entertainment industry.

Who networks?

Nearly every person who has a modicum of success in the entertainment industry finds that networking is a vital and integral part of their life — from studio execs to agents, from producers to writers, from assistants to those who would like to be part of this crazy business. Any serious screenwriter who would like their latest script to be read for representation by an agent or for consideration as a project by a production company should look upon networking as a natural offshoot of their writing talent.

Why is networking so important?

Networking, along with talent (be it acting, directing, writing, dealmaking, producing, etc.), is the lifeblood of the entertainment industry. Cultivating relationships can lead to unexpected opportunities. Networking, when properly done, can be informative, productive, and will often lead to friendship as well as some helpful door-opening.

WARNING: Successful networking is based upon mutual respect. One-sided, self-serving relationships are strongly discouraged.

Preparation.

If you are planning to attend a conference, pitchfest or film festival, here are some pre-event pointers to keep in mind:

> Read the conference brochure or program thoroughly, paying careful attention to the faculty members or the special guests who will be attending. Most brochures or programs include a brief biographical sketch. If bios are not included, do not be afraid to call the organization that is putting on the event to ask for brief credentials on the speakers.

> Select two or three speakers or guests whose credentials are in line with your needs and interests. In other words, if you have just completed a comedy about a family that is lost in space, it would be more productive to focus on meeting the producer or studio exec who has worked on a family feature, rather than the independent filmmaker who specializes in low-budget horror films. Note that I have suggested keying in on two or three guests. While some overzealous writers may want to meet and greet every single faculty member, it is unwise to spend every minute of the conference or festival networking and lose out on gathering valuable information from the workshops.

> If you are unfamiliar with someone's credits, do some research. *The Hollywood Creative Directory*, *Video Hound Golden Movie Retriever*, *The Internet Movie Database*, and *Leonard Maltin's Movie Guide* are very helpful resources to use, especially if you want to find out about the unfamiliar film that a producer worked on. If you are planning to speak with a producer, network exec, television writer or showrunner, his credits might be found in *The Complete Directory to Prime Time Network and Cable TV Shows*. Doing a search online can usually deliver film reviews or additional information about the production company, studio or agency. Some resourceful writers have found it helpful to view

the speaker's past work on video, providing additional topics of conversation when networking with them or other attendees.

> Read the trade papers for up-to-the-minute information. Become familiar with common terms used in the entertainment industry. Be sure and scan the weekly film and television production sections of the trades, noting which companies or studios are doing family-oriented projects and might be future production houses to target when you complete your new kid's adventure film. Take careful note of projects that mention faculty members (producers, writers, etc., are complimented when someone mentions their latest work).

> Carefully plan your schedule to include those workshops, panels, screenings and sessions which will be most appropriate and in line with your interests. Accept the fact that you will never be everywhere at once. Just a warning: Workshop-hopping can be hazardous. Listening to half of a session will probably only give you half the picture, and may end up confusing rather than enlightening you. Jot down some questions that pertain to the workshops or the panels you have selected. Hopefully, the speaker or panelists will be able to address those questions during the session. If the question was thought-provoking, it may also be a point of discussion, should you happen to see that speaker later during the event.

> If the conference allows, take advantage of scheduling a consultation with one or more of the faculty or workshop speakers. Keep in mind, however, that there are a limited number of both consultations and faculty members. Try to be flexible by giving conference organizers three or four choices of faculty members. Also, be aware that speakers may only be available at certain time periods, which might mean missing part of another session. Most attendees will agree that, if given a choice between attending a workshop and having a ten-minute consultation, the consultation would be the best bet. Most importantly, many conferences will assign consultations based on early registration;

whichever attendees register first will most likely get their preferred choice of a prized consultation.

While attending the event.

> If you were unable to obtain a consultation with a speaker, be sure to check with the conference staff for possible cancellations. Often, you will be put on a waiting list.

> Remember that networking can be done throughout the conference or the festival. Many conferences set aside specific times that are particularly geared for interaction between special guests and event attendees. However, some networking can be done between workshops and during meals, as long as common courtesy is shown (i.e., if a speaker is seated at your table during lunch, please allow them to finish their lunch before bombarding them with questions). And as always, ask one question at a time, allowing other participants to speak as well.

> If a speaker or panelist has not covered a specific area, or if you are unclear about a point he has addressed, do not be shy about raising your hand and asking questions or asking for further clarification. All questions should be asked in a courteous and non-combative manner. One writer, eager to prove a point and hopefully get himself noticed, did so in a brash and aggressive manner, which did not endear him to the panelists or the members of the audience. When he later ran into the speaker at the event party, the speaker was only coolly polite. The writer quickly realized his brashness was a mistake.

Additional networking hints.

> Remember to network with other attendees. Some writers are so busy pursuing faculty members that they overlook the more lasting value of networking with other writers and conference attendees. Most events supply badges or nametags with the attendees' names and sometimes their hometowns. If you have been looking for a screenwriting critique group, it would be

very beneficial to network with others who live in your general area. If you happen to strike up a friendship with another writer, perhaps you both could pool your notes. If you have a consultation with a speaker or have a scheduling conflict, doing a little shared networking could produce an offer to make a copy of an audio tape or notes on the missed session. Several writers have found writing partners by networking at an event.

> Learn to ask questions that require more than just a simple "Yes" or "No" answer. As successful businesspersons in marketing and sales will tell you, it is important to master the art of asking open-ended questions — e.g., "What do you think about...", "How would you feel if...", etc. Asking open-ended questions can also result in a more thorough answer and also gives others the impression that you are genuinely interested in their advice, comments and/or opinions.

> During a workshop, panel or question-and-answer session, it is advisable to confine your questions to the specific area covered (i.e., if the workshop is about TV sitcoms, it would be preferable not to ask about dramatic structure). In general, attendees might want to raise specific questions regarding their personal projects during a consultation with a faculty member rather than during a workshop. If, however, a producer has mentioned that he has a particular interest in an arena that coincides with your project, you can always mention it after the Q&A session if the opportunity presents itself. There are no guarantees that the producer, exec or agent will ask to see your script, but it is a way of relaying the information. If the producer is amenable, he may contact you during the conference. If you are shy or if there is not enough time to get to you before the session ends, it is perfectly acceptable to talk with the speaker or panelist between workshops or sessions or during a networking opportunity as long as the speaker is not hurrying off to another scheduled commitment.

> If you are fortunate enough to have a consultation with a faculty member, be fully prepared with a few key questions. Starting

out a consultation by handing an agent your script and asking him to represent you is not the suggested way to network. Instead, give the agent a little background on yourself. If you have published works in other areas of writing, mention that. If you have more than one script (always "music" to an agent's ears), give a log line on each to see if it piques his interest, remembering that agents want writers who are in for the long haul and have screenplays they can sell. If your consultation is with a producer or studio exec, they are more likely to be impressed if you ask about their future development slate or if their projects must meet specific budgetary demands. Keep in mind that most studio execs are unable to accept submissions unless they come from a producer, agent or entertainment attorney. Consultations with studio execs and producers can give writers valuable information about the types of projects studios are looking for or what actors and directors have production deals with them. Whether the faculty member is an agent, producer, exec, writer or consultant, attendees can always find out more about the industry marketplace and any discernable turn-ons or turn-offs.

> Remember that the most successful networking is when both parties receive shared benefits. Like friendships and marriages, the best networking relationships survive when there is give and take on both sides, coupled with a healthy and genuine dose of mutual respect.

> As Forrest Gump would say, "My mama always told me to say *please* and *thank you*." If a fellow attendee, speaker or workshop leader was especially helpful or made a positive impression on you — either during his workshop, consultation or at a networking event — you may want to send a brief follow-up note of thanks. This approach is another way to extend your networking once the conference or event has concluded. If you did not receive a business card, you can always address your "thank you" note to the organization that sponsored the event and they will pass it on.

> Post-conference, continue to keep in touch with other conference attendees who were helpful and shared similar writing and life philosophies. This practice greatly increases the opportunities for mutual benefit if one of you should become successful. With the Internet, there is absolutely no reason why you cannot stay in touch! As one writer mentioned to me, "It's great to have an understanding shoulder to cry on when you get writer's block."

> Be generous to others in the hopes that what goes around, comes around. Do not be shy about letting others know of your success. It provides hope and encouragement to all. Greet and speak to others using direct eye contact and always remember that a friendly smile goes a long way.

Networking *faux pas.*

Here are some actual examples of what **not** to do where networking is concerned.

Crossing the line.

Not long ago, I received a call from an agent who had participated on a panel with me. He started out the conversation: "So you think this writer has potential, huh? She said she was one of your students and was sending me her screenplay at your suggestion." Much as I tried, I couldn't recall this writer (let's call her Dawn). I had to set the record straight.

While Dawn may have taken one of my classes or workshops, I had not personally recommended her to this agent or any other agent. This overzealous writer, whose effort may sound creative to some, had crossed the line and, in doing so, may have done herself more harm than good.

It is important to understand that the entertainment industry is built on networking relationships and personal favors. While some writers may get away with half-truths and finger-crossing, most will do better by not starting off on the wrong side of the line. Clearly Dawn had not expected the agent to call me.

I wish this had been a one-time occurrence, but similar scenarios occur at least three or four times a year. Unfortunately, this kind of thing happens to many of my colleagues in the industry as well.

Here is an example of a better alternative for Dawn.

Dawn should schedule a ten-minute consultation with the agent at the conference. During the consultation, she should ask the agent about the marketplace. What genres are selling? Which studios/production companies are looking for strong, character-driven dramas (or whatever is the focus of Dawn's latest project)? She should query the agent about how large the agency is and what kind of writing talent its agents are looking for.

Armed with information she has gathered from the trade papers, Dawn could then discuss her latest work that might be appropriate for a particular star (who just happens to be a client of this agency).

Perhaps at a networking session during the event, Dawn could re-connect with the agent and mention other projects she is working on that might tie in with information brought up during other sessions or workshops. Her approach would show initiative and let the agent know that she is not only productive but takes her writing seriously.

The one-sided opportunist.

One overly eager writer (we'll call him Tom) asked if he could sit in on a writers' group session to see if he would fit in. During the session, he spoke with an up-and-coming writer whose screenplay had just been optioned by a noted producer. Tom asked the writer if she would introduce him to this producer. The writer said she would be happy to "when the time was right."

Tom promptly sent his script to the producer, using the writer's name as his entry. Obviously, he felt the time was right *now*. You can imagine the writer's embarrassment when the producer called several weeks later to say that Tom's work was mediocre and totally inappropriate for his company. Tom, by the way, only attended that one meeting of the writers group and never returned, having gotten what he thought he came for: a possible key contact. However, he left a potential colleague with egg on her face and she will probably be unwilling to help him out again.

Here's how Tom could have approached things in a more productive and professional way:

Tom sits in on the writers group and spends the first half of the meeting listening carefully, assessing personalities, and discovering where the various members are in their writing (absolute beginner, more experienced writer with work optioned, someone with sample scripts who wants an agent, etc.). Tom also gauges his own comfort level within the group.

During a break, Tom chats with at least two members. Then, if he is comfortable, he begins participating actively in the rest of the session, but only if he has constructive comments to make. This approach allows the rest of the group to get to know him. If his contributions are helpful and positive, it is likely he will fit in.

Once invited to join, Tom attends the writers group for a few months, getting to know the members and allowing them to get to know him as well. When he learns that certain members have agents or have had the good fortune to get material read or optioned, he asks them for advice on how he might achieve similar results.

With this approach, members of the group will most likely want to help Tom. They will probably want to read his work before they refer him to a producer or agent. This is standard procedure whenever a writer asks anyone in the industry (be it exec, producer, agent, etc.) for a favor or referral. The person extending the favor has to know and believe in your work because their reputation is on the line with every recommendation.

Some real-life results.

In their desperation to be recognized and to achieve their goals, over-zealous writers like Dawn and Tom failed to recognize and acknowledge the following:

> The film and television industry is a relatively small community where no one is more than one person away from knowing someone else.

> The industry thrives on networking and the relationship among agents, producers, directors, actors, writers, consultants and executives is not be to taken lightly.

> Because this community is so very close-knit, a considerable amount of news is shared and traded, including information, gossip, and occasionally stories like the two I just shared.

> It is often said that a person in this industry is only as good as his or her last movie, last role, last script, or last *faux pas*!

Making the most of favors.

As is the case in any line of work, those with the power to hire prefer one quality person to ten mediocre ones. This opinion is especially true in the entertainment industry. Therefore, recommendations and favors are to be taken seriously and are not given out to everyone.

If you are fortunate enough to be given a true opportunity, think of it as the only favor this person may ever grant you. Value what you have been given (no matter what the outcome) and be certain that the work you submit is at its best and will not embarrass you or the person recommending you. And, most of all, remember that sharing your knowledge and opportunities with others is part of the process.

Chapter 12

You Are Not Alone: Group Therapy For Writers

(aka Getting The Most Out Of Writing Conferences And Writers' Groups)

One of the best examples of a writers group in action happened at a conference a few years ago. Three members of a writing group each attended a different workshop held during the same time period. They took notes at each class and were armed with a set of questions that they asked during each presentation's Q&A period. I would see the three individuals gathering during the breaks between workshops. One of them would take all the notes, make copies at the hotel business office, and then deliver them to each of the other writers at the next break. Curious, I caught up with the group during dinner and found out they had studied the conference schedule and divided up the workshops. They had also looked at the description of each workshop and had each submitted a question that they wanted answered at that workshop. Their coordinated efforts even extended to the next day's pitchfest, where they gave each other bits of information they had learned from their individual pitches — e.g., "Agency A specializes in writers for television only," "Production Company B is looking for a teen comedy," "Exec C said her studio just signed a first-look deal with Director D."

When I caught up with them after the pitchfest, they had succeeded in having requests for treatments or scripts from a total of twelve entities. This group gave new meaning to Sun Tzu's Art of War strategy "to divide and conquer."

One of the best ways to take away the self-doubt that most writers put upon themselves from time to time is to meet other writers. "But where?" you ask. Why not attend a writing conference where you can meet other writers and also make valuable industry contacts, sharpen your creative skills, and expand your education as a writer? Or why not consider joining or starting a writers' group in your area or online?

In the past several years, more pitchfests and conferences have featured screenwriting as a major focus or the sole focus of their event. From Seattle to Michigan, from Austin to Hawaii, from Vancouver to Santa Fe, universities, film commissions and large networks of writers are sponsoring screenwriting days, pitchfests, and weekend conferences. While admission to these events can be anywhere from free to several hundred dollars, they can be a productive and beneficial way for screenwriters to get connected and stay connected.

Getting ready.

If you have made the decision to attend one of these events, prepare yourself mentally. While it is a good idea to establish goals for yourself, be realistic. Know in advance that there are no guaranteed rules for breaking into screenwriting. "Overnight successes" are most assuredly the exception rather than the rule.

At conferences speakers, panelists and consultants each offer their own set of guidelines, methods or advice that have worked for them. As most of us should be wise enough to know, what works for one person will not necessarily work for all. However, advice and information should always be greeted with an open mind and respect for the person who is sharing his knowledge with you and the other writers in attendance.

Here is some preparation you can do in advance:

> Read the conference brochure carefully and decide your schedule. If the conference offers first-come first-served appointments with faculty members, be sure to sign up early to avoid disappointment.

> Review the brochure and select the workshops and panels that are appropriate for your level of experience. Plan to attend classes that will sharpen your skills and/or benefit your particular area of interest (or weakness), such as character development, structure, television/cable movies, sitcoms, etc. If two interesting workshops are scheduled at the same time, make a note to look for someone you can share notes with — someone who will attend one session while you attend the other.

> If you have special needs (such as dietary requirements for meals, a handicapped-accessible room, etc.), you will want to read the conference material carefully to see if these needs are addressed. If you do not see the information you need, do not be shy about calling the conference organizers to ask if these requests can be handled in advance.

> Make a checklist of materials to bring to the conference: laptop, flash drives, notepads, writing instruments, business cards (if you have them), tape recorder, tapes and batteries (always check in advance with conference personnel or speakers to find out if taping is allowed). If you are feeling particularly optimistic, you might want to bring along a copy or two of your treatment or script, and if you plan on pitching, bring along some copies of your P.O.P.

> If you arrive early, check out the areas where your workshops will be held. Be sure to note where conference rooms are located in relation to one another and to the registration desk, dining area, and rest rooms.

> During registration, ask conference staff members if there are any last-minute changes not listed on the program (such as cancelled workshops, substitute speakers, room changes, etc.). If applicable, you may want to adjust your own schedule accordingly.

Attending sessions.

During a workshop, make it a point to sit as close to the front of the room as you can — especially if you plan to tape the session and take accurate notes. Depending on the size of the room, the speaker may not use a microphone. If you are sitting at the back, you may spend a great deal of effort in straining to hear the speaker; if you are trying to tape the session, your recorder will be less than effective.

Many regular workshop leaders enjoy communicating with the audience, an effort that is much harder to achieve if the audience is scattered all over the room. If you know in advance that you may have to leave a session early (say, for a one-on-one meeting), select a seat next to the aisle and closer to the door.

Of course, you will want to comply with all conference guidelines or rules. These are usually stated in the conference program or posted at the registration desk, or mentioned at the start of the event. They include things like wearing nametags or badges at all times, not smoking or eating in the conference rooms, or not taping a session without asking a speaker's permission. If a speaker declines your request to tape a session, it might be due to one of two possibilities. The speaker may work for a large company or corporation that will not allow them to be taped, or the speaker may be an author whose audio and visual rights are under contract to the publisher.

Be aware that, with few exceptions, all sessions must begin and end on time to prevent a domino effect that could throw the entire day's conference schedule off.

Workshop courtesy.

Here are some suggestions to help you get the most out of each workshop that you attend:

> Feel free to ask questions, especially during the question-and-answer period at the end of a workshop. If you do not understand a particular point made by the speaker, raise your hand and ask for further explanation. Few presenters mind valid interruptions, and chances are there may be someone else in the room who also needs clarification.

> Try not to monopolize a speaker's time by asking more than one question, especially if there are others who have their hand raised. Also, address speakers and fellow participants in a positive manner, even if your thoughts and comments are not in line with theirs.

> During seminars, be sure to state your questions succinctly and clearly so that everyone can hear. Prepare specific questions in advance for each of the workshops you will be attending. If your question is not answered during the speaker's formal presentation, take advantage of the question-and-answer session that usually follows.

> When a workshop comes to a close, refrain from crowding the speaker when they are leaving the stage/podium area. Keep in mind that the room usually needs to be cleared and readied for the next workshop. Also, inadvertently holding a speaker "at bay" makes it difficult for them to stay on schedule.

> Most workshops provide adequate time to ask questions at the end of a session. If, for some reason, you were unable to ask yours, wait until the speaker has left the classroom before you ask. If the speaker does not have to rush off to another commitment, they should be happy to answer your query. In return, do not try to turn the answer into a personal consultation.

Networking courtesy.

Probably one of the highlights of many of the writing conferences is the networking events that enable faculty members and speakers to mingle with the attendees. In addition to any one-on-one appointments you are fortunate enough to obtain, networking get-togethers are your golden opportunity to make contacts and gather information.

> If you want to ask a question during such an event, make a good impression by politely waiting your turn and keeping your question brief and to the point. Remember that other participants are eagerly awaiting their turns, too.

> While it is great to be assertive, no one appreciates people who ungraciously monopolize a speaker's time, rudely interrupt others, or go overboard by not respecting a speaker's privacy. I once witnessed a writer at a conference who was so desperate to have her script read that she followed an agent into the women's restroom and pushed her script under the stall door. Needless to say, the agent firmly rejected this act, and the writer was told by conference personnel to keep a respectful distance from the agent or she would be asked to leave.

> If you are lucky enough to obtain a one-on-one appointment with a speaker, plan your agenda in advance. Determine three to five questions you want to ask, keeping in mind that most appointments last a mere ten minutes and, at some events, only five minutes. If you opt to pitch your project during a one-on-one, practice in advance — again, keeping a careful eye on the clock. If your appointment is ten minutes, allow five minutes for your pitch and five minutes for feedback from the speaker. If your appointment is only five minutes, allow three minutes for the pitch and two minutes for feedback.

> Because of time restrictions, it is unwise to ask a speaker to read a few scenes or a synopsis of your work and to make comments. Also, be aware that many agents, executives and producers cannot accept your screenplay at a conference — mostly for legal reasons, but also for logistical ones (few speakers have enough room in their suitcases to lug home forty scripts).

> Carefully consider which key presenters you would like to meet during the networking events. If there is a producer who specializes in family entertainment and you have a "boy and his dog" project, you would be wise to put this speaker at the top of your networking list. If your latest comedy is perfect for Adam Sandler, make it a point to speak with the development exec whose studio has a deal with the comedian.

Additional advice.

The following are additional suggestions and advice from veterans of writers' conferences:

> If you are unable to obtain an appointment with a particular speaker, try asking a conference staff member to put you on a waiting list in case of a cancellation. Then be sure that staff members know where you will be in case they need to reach you. Conversely, if you are unable to keep an appointment, let conference personnel know as soon as possible so they can give someone else the opportunity to meet and query the speaker.

> Type A personalities will probably ignore this, but consider making time to relax during a conference. These events provide so much information packed into such a brief span of time that a break should be considered a mandatory part of your schedule. You might take a short walk between sessions or go to your room for a brief nap. If your schedule offers absolutely no time for breaks during the day, be sure to allow plenty of time to rest at the end of each evening. You might want to take fifteen minutes before bed to quietly evaluate what you've absorbed.

> It is an unfortunate fact that the roster of speakers at conferences is subject to change. Even though it is the goal of conference organizers to make every effort to maintain workshops and speakers as originally planned, there are times when changes are necessary and unavoidable. Instead of letting such changes throw you off course, re-evaluate your goals and seek out other opportunities and contacts.

> If there is a situation that deserves immediate action (such as not enough handouts, not enough seats, etc.), seek out a staff member to rectify the situation.

> Most conferences provide evaluation forms that give you a forum for your suggestions or complaints. If your experience was a positive one, you may want to introduce yourself to the conference director or a staff member to express your praise in

person. In any case, do take the time to express your thoughts on the evaluation form. Let conference leaders know which events and/or faculty members were outstanding. Conversely, if you were disappointed with a workshop, explain why the session did not meet your expectations. These commentaries are valuable tools for planning future conferences; your feedback may ensure that your needs and those of the others attending will be met.

> In addition to networking with faculty members, do not forget to network with the other writers attending. Writing is such a solitary art, many find it extremely beneficial to share their experiences with others who are also waiting for the "big break." Participants at past conferences have ended up forming critique groups, sharing and comparing workshop notes, and have benefited from an exchange of knowledge by pooling information.

Group therapy.

As stated earlier, a growing phenomenon among writers (novelists and nonfiction scribes as well as screenwriters) is joining a writers group or critique group. Although writing, on the surface, seems to be primarily a solo effort, you will find that what happens during the writing, as well as after your write "FADE OUT," is actually a collaborative effort. Screenwriters, especially those starting out, can benefit greatly from joining a writers group.

Discovering some of the benefits.

One of the toughest things a new writer faces is staying focused on the work at hand. When you only have *you* to answer to, it is sometimes tempting to go off track. Belonging to a group that shares a common desire to put pen to paper (or keyboard to inkjet) goes a very long way toward keeping you committed, disciplined, and focused keenly on your writing.

Another obvious benefit of belonging to a group is the ability to share information, problems, and possible solutions. You would be surprised how many areas of concern all writers share. There is the old nemesis, writer's block, as well as self-doubt, lack of motivation, and creating a more exciting ending for Act Two — to name a few.

In addition to offering suggestions to enhance a group member's work, those writers who band together also give emotional support, encouragement, and, as one writer told me, have even given members a job during the lean and discouraging times that often occur. Many successful writers have benefited from participating in a writers group early in their careers.

Another benefit can be financial in nature. Imagine how much money can be saved if a group of people chip in to buy, circulate and share materials such as copies of notable screenplays, reference materials, a subscription to a trade paper, etc. A subscription to *Variety* or *The Hollywood Reporter* can set you back a few hundred dollars a year. But imagine dividing that cost by four or five people? *The Hollywood Creative Directory* is about $65 per edition. But for less than $13 each, five people can share the cost.

One of the greatest benefits, however, is the power of networking. It is not uncommon for a successful member to help another talented writer by introducing his or her work to an agent, producer or executive. Such help is encouraged because the entertainment industry is fickle, and no one knows when your time in the spotlight may shift and you will need the support of others. Also, the genuine friendship and respect that develops amongst writers is probably one of the best perks of all.

Discovering some of the benefits.

First of all, it is advisable for members of a writers group to be "geographically desirable" if possible. However, with the advent of the Internet, there are dozens of writing and critique groups that have been in operation for several years online, making its member's geographical locations irrelevant. Also, it is fairly easy to find chat rooms for screenwriters and to form groups from there.

If you prefer meeting your group in person (the preference of many writers), it can be as easy as attending a writers' conference or a pitchfest and talking to other attendees. As mentioned earlier, many of the conferences encourage such networking by adding the hometown under the participant's name on their badge. One past pitchfest veteran told me that he saw a plea on the message board of the pitchfest that read: "Am I the only person in the Lansing, Michigan, area who is writing screenplays?" By the end of the conference, there were four people who lived within an hour's drive who had contacted him, and a writers group was instantly formed.

If you are taking a writing or film class at a local university or college, consider bringing up the idea of a writing or critique group in your class. Other possibilities might include posting inquiries at bookstores or gathering information from little theater groups, drama or literature classes, film societies, film festival offices, state or city film commissions, or friends and family who may have acquaintances or neighbors who have expressed an interest in screenwriting.

It is helpful, but not mandatory, to have members at relatively the same stage of development or writing knowledge. It is also advisable to limit the number of participants so everyone will get the opportunity to have his or her work presented and critiqued on a regular basis. If a large number of writers wish to join, division by writing experience is a possible solution: for example, beginners, those with a screenplay already started, those with at least one script completed, etc.

Set up a mutually agreeable date and time for your meetings. Groups can meet bimonthly, once a month, or even once a quarter. Make sure your meeting place has comfortable seating and will be relatively free of disturbances. Meeting at a restaurant is fine if management does not mind and the restaurant has a small room that is separate from the main dining areas. Meeting in someone's home is ideal if there is room for all members. Libraries, bookstores, colleges and universities, and occasionally banks and shopping malls will have "community rooms" that they open up to community groups.

Establishing guidelines.

Now that your group has agreed where and how often to meet, you should next decide to develop a mutual agenda. Some groups use the meetings exclusively for critiquing, while others make room for sharing writing-related information they have come across since the last meeting. Some groups focus on the work of one or two members per meeting, especially if the group has more than five or six members.

The group needs to agree that each member will write a certain number of pages or scenes before the next time they are to meet. At each meeting, make sure there are enough copies of each member's work for each person present. Decide if the work will be sent to members in advance of the meeting (either by snail mail, email, or fax) or if time will be set aside for reading during the meeting.

Some of the more successful writers groups assign a group leader to remind others of meetings and to keep the discussion on track. Rotate this position periodically to avoid overburdening any one particular member.

When you have something to contribute, you must also be fully prepared to participate. Always be honest in your praise and constructive in your criticism. When commenting, try to put yourself in the recipient's shoes; unnecessarily harsh criticisms, petty remarks and personal judgments have no place in these discussions. Be open-minded to the opinions and suggestions of others, and they will usually show you the same well-deserved respect.

Always be on time. Everyone's time is valuable. And be sure that your work is ready. Are there enough copies? Is your work legible and in proper form? Be sure to "pass the spotlight" on to others by not taking more than your share of the time allotted for each person's work.

Consider setting aside some time at the end of each meeting for members to share good news, writing-related or otherwise. If the group is especially close, you can share bad news as well. One writer told me that if it were not for her passion for writing and the pep talks given to her by members of her group, she might not have made it through her divorce. But never lose sight of the purpose of the group: to support and encourage one another's writing efforts. Try to keep the "green-eyed monster" under control. If someone gets an option or an agent, be gracious and celebrate their success — you never know when that member might help you to make a valuable connection.

Finally, it is crucial that all members remember the cardinal rule of all writers' groups: Keep all materials and discussions completely confidential.

Knowing when to leave.

While some relationships survive through the worst of storms, there may come a time when you feel a need to leave your writers group. Perhaps the group has lost its focus or has veered from its original goal of supporting members' writing ambitions. Or maybe an unforeseen personal problem in your life must take precedence over your writing. Change is understandable. If you feel you are falling behind or if you cannot carry through on your responsibilities to the other members of the group, do not be afraid to leave the group or ask if you can take a temporary break.

If you suddenly find Lady Fortune smiling down on you and you have more writing assignments than you can handle, you will likely be too busy to stay in a writers group. Yet, one of the greatest benefits of such a group is the friendships that can form through the years. I know of one group of writers who are all doing well — two of them are TV staff writers, one is a highly successful writer/director, and two have had some produced work — yet they still continue to meet each month — to play poker and kick around story ideas between antes.

Chapter 13

A Word To The Wise:
Agents, Lawyers, Consultants,
And Other Possible Disasters

Cautionary tale: Are you aware that many writers have been known to zealously protect their screenplays by putting a copy in the freezer in case of a fire? Unfortunately, one writer's neighborhood suffered a twenty-four-hour power outage. It wasn't until a day later that she discovered that her beloved script had been reduced to a soggy mess.

Once you have written a script, you are likely to be looking for someone who can help you to take your work to market. But who should you turn to? An agent? An entertainment attorney? A manager? A script consultant? How best can you protect your work?

What is an "agent"?

Next to your own writing talent, a good agent can be a writer's greatest asset. An agent represents you by presenting your work to a variety of entertainment industry entities, such as studios, production companies, networks and cable companies.

What can an agent do for me?

Good agents can save you a lot of precious time, energy and expense by doing most of the marketing you would have to do if you were not represented. They can open doors with ease if they have made solid contacts at major production venues. They keep their contacts current with frequent phone calls, lunches, and/or visits to query about the types of projects being sought and to ask about writing assignments that need to be filled.

When you are stuck on a project, a good agent can serve as a sounding board — offering advice, encouragement, and constructive criticism. Good agents can do research on your behalf when it comes time for negotiations. They know when to take the initiative to push ahead, but above all, they know never to walk away from a fair deal.

Do I need an agent?

If you live out of the Southern California area and do not have the finances to afford travel expenses, monthly phone, postage and courier bills, nor the time to spend writing and marketing yourself, then the answer is that you would be better off with an agent.

Having an agent in the Los Angeles area (or at least an agent who is a signatory to the Writers Guild of America) guarantees that you will be represented by someone who is fully cognizant of the professional guidelines and courtesies that exist in the entertainment industry. In other words, a good agent knows how to do business in the entertainment community. This is especially important if you, the agent's client, live outside the greater Los Angeles area.

Sheer economics is also a major ongoing factor to consider. Frequent phone calls, airfare, hotel accommodations, and business lunches and dinners are expensive but accepted ways for agents to establish solid relationships with each of their contacts. Good agents have dozens, sometimes hundreds, of professional contacts at different venues. Keeping up on the needs of these contacts while matching those needs with the talents and abilities of their represented writers is not always an easy task.

Yes, there are a few writers who do not have agents and manage to do well. But most of them had an agent to get them started on the road to a successful career. Also, if further queried, many of those un-agented writers would have to admit that instead of an agent, they have high-powered entertainment attorneys or business managers to represent them, all of whom demand hefty annual retainers, plus any incurred legal costs.

How much does an agent get?

Agents who are signatories to the Writers Guild of America get the same fee — 10% of a writer's gross earnings. It cannot be stressed enough: Do not retain an agent who is not WGA-affiliated, and never give any money up front to an agent, even if the agent claims to be WGA-affiliated.

Why should the agent be WGA-affiliated?

Unfortunately, there are dozens of horror stories I have heard — mostly from out-of-area writers who were conned out of hundreds, sometimes thousands, of dollars by so-called "agents" who were not WGA-approved. If you are not sure whether an agent is a WGA signatory, simply contact the Writers Guild of America West (*wga.org*) and ask for a list of agents who are signatories to the WGA.

How do I get an agent?

This is probably the question I'm most frequently asked.

The very best way to get an agent is if you have a connection who can refer you. A connection can mean a friend, relative, business associate, or casual acquaintance. A writer I know got her script to an agent because her apartment manager happened to mention that he played tennis with one agent. She cooked a spaghetti dinner for the apartment manager who gave the script to his tennis partner who eventually became the writer's first agent.

If you do not have a connection for a referral, the best place to start is by logging onto the WGA website and clicking onto the section regarding agents. There will be instructions on how to request their approved agency list. Although the numbers are small, some agencies (even some that say they aren't accepting submissions) will accept material from new writers. If you send a query to one of these agencies, remember to enclose a SASE. It is helpful to begin working on your next script while you wait for a response. It may take weeks (yes, even months) for agents to work their way through the piles of correspondence sent to them.

What is included in a query letter?

In your query letter, keep things brief and to the point. The query letter should never be more than a page long. You should start off your letter with a hook — your project's title, the genre, and a winning paragraph that gives the agent (or producer or exec) a reason to want to read your project. If your project is for animation, make that clear. If your material is based on a true story or is adapted from another medium, be sure to indicate this.

Next, if you are a published writer, or if you have placed or won a screenwriting competition or were part of a scriptwriting fellowship program, you can then briefly mention this. If you attended film school, you can mention that as well.

If you have more than one script, do not be afraid to tell them, "I have two completed comedy scripts and am working on my third." This statement indicates that you are not a one-script wonder and that you are genuinely interested in a full-time career as a screenwriter.

And if your project was inspired by your work or an experience you once had, do not be afraid to indicate this — it can be a plus for you.

One agent told me her interest was piqued when an emerging screenwriter sent her a query letter in which he mentioned that he was a former FBI agent who had to quit the Bureau because of a work-related injury. Since his log line stated that the hero of his script is an FBI agent who uncovers a covert espionage squad within the government, the literary agent was immediately intrigued and asked to see the script.

One observation I have found puzzling after reading thousands of submission queries is that writers tend to dash off very generic, almost sterile letters that do not show much in the way of a personal writing style. Screenwriters often forget that the first sample of their writing that agents, managers, producers or execs will read is their cover or query letter. If that first piece of writing lacks style and creativity, chances are good that a potential agent or producer may not be impressed enough to request your script.

Here is a sample query letter which might have tempted Warner Bros. to take on the hit movie *The Blind Side*:

Name of Recipient
Address of Production Company, Studio or Network

Your Name
Your Address
Your Email Address
Your Phone Number

Date

Dear —

"The Blind Side" is an inspirational family drama based on the dramatic and emotionally compelling true story based on the book, *The Blind Side: Evolution of a Game*, by Michael Lewis. I have negotiated the film rights to the book, which focuses on Baltimore Ravens offensive lineman Michael Oher, who, as a homeless black teen finds his tragic life turned around when he is adopted by a loving, wealthy, white family. Leigh Anne Touhy is the driving force behind giving Michael first a home, then love, then a future, both in terms of his education and a career. Together, she and Michael bond as they fight the prejudice of some of her privileged friends and the low expectations that the school has for him. Fueled by Leigh Anne's faith and Michael's sense of humor and self-respect, he becomes a member of the Tuohy family, which includes a teenage daughter and young son.

I'd like to submit "The Blind Side" for your consideration. My credits as a screenwriter are attached. (Or, if you have no credits, mention any writing contests you've done well in, if you've gone to film school or any professional writing experience you have in other areas.) I have one other completed script and am currently working on a mystery-thriller.

If you would like to read "The Blind Side," you can reach me at the above address or phone number. Thank you for your time and consideration.

Sincerely,

Your Name

What do I do if I do not get a positive response?

Your second line of action should be the library, local bookstore, or the Internet. Request or order *The Hollywood Creative Directory*. It is updated a few times each year, but you (or your writers group) may want to consider purchasing this reference manual once a year.

When you receive your directory, read the entries carefully, noting which companies specialize in television or features. Be aware that most major studios and larger production companies have strongly enforced legal policies regarding unsolicited submissions and will usually return material unread.

However, many successful writers have gotten their start by using what I call the "back door method." It is a well-known fact in Hollywood that many of the smaller production companies are more flexible about accepting submissions from non-represented writers who will sign a standard release form (see page 185 for more information on release forms). Often, the smaller companies will only option a project, rather than buy it outright. Still, many writers have secured an option and then asked a contact at the production company to suggest a possible agent.

If an agent knows you have proven talent (the option), he may be more open to looking at you as a potential client, especially if you let him know that you have more than one script with several other ideas in the works. The agent, who wants to be in business with the production company, will usually take a look at your script if it is referred to him by a development exec at the company. This is part of the unwritten favor system of networking which has been in existence for decades. This is a clear-cut example of how networking in The Biz pays off.

Are there other options?

Other helpful resources are *The Hollywood Scriptwriter*, *Scr(i)pt* magazine, and *Creative Screenwriting* magazine. Each of these resources devotes an issue annually to the subject of agents and agencies and how to open the doors to representation.

Also, websites like MovieBytes, InkTip, and the European website TwelvePoint often list helpful links (to production companies, agencies, and even foreign production entities) that may prove useful.

What do agents look for in clients?

Agents look for focused and determined writers. They want writers who are in for the long haul. A writer should have at least two or three scripts to show, with outlines or treatments for at least another one or two. In addition to the obvious factor of talent, agents want clients who have work that will sell, so at least one or two of your scripts should be for a mainstream audience (comedy, romance, action, adventure, family, mystery/thriller).

This advice is not meant to stifle your creative talent, but is said with the knowledge that the more potential buyers your agent can present your screenplays to, the greater your exposure. On the other hand, a well-written script that is smaller in focus, more unusual, and not mainstream, only needs one buyer; a good agent who recognizes your gem will work diligently to find the right buyer.

Agents are not much different from producers and studio execs. They, too, want fully developed characters, strong structure, solid dialogue, with an attention-getting writing style that is generally spare but also creative, visual, and telling. As one of my favorite agents once quipped, "It's also a plus if a writer client is patient, open-minded and flexible."

Which agency is best?

Agents and agencies are to be viewed like all business partners — with a combination of suspicion and hope. Some are ultimately better than others. However, once you have an agent, if that person turns out not to be a good fit for you, you can always part with them (if they have not found work for you after a specified time span) and attempt to secure another agent. Some writers have managed to query the interest of other agents before actually making the split from the first agency. But this type of maneuver must be handled carefully; a less experienced writer could find himself being dropped altogether and without anyone to represent him if he is not careful.

For writers who are new in the business, it is best to start with the smaller literary agencies, the ones that are mentioned in the WGA list of agencies who are willing to look at unsolicited material.

Why not the big, splashy, headline-getting agencies who make those million-dollar deals? Most of those mega-agencies only have clients who have already established a name and a solid career for themselves by having at least one or two produced movies. Also, most of those mega-agencies focus more on packaging projects by taking a client's script and putting a director and/or acting talent from the same agency so the agency can then claim fees from the writer, director, and the actor. And, more importantly, mega-agencies do not always have the time that is necessary to help an emerging writer with his struggling career.

What is an "entertainment attorney"?

An **entertainment attorney** can perform tasks similar to an agent. They will often be willing to submit material to their contacts at different production houses and studios. The biggest difference, however, is that they are not bound to the WGA. Therefore, entertainment attorneys can charge as little as 5% to as much as 20% or more if they are able to submit and sell one of your screenplays. Some attorneys will charge additional fees for negotiating contracts and submitting scripts.

If you are interested in obtaining an attorney to represent you, you will need to ask the following questions:

> How long has the attorney done business in the entertainment industry?

> Is she an independent attorney or is she part of a larger law firm?

> What is needed to hire her as your representative?

> Does she require an annual retainer or does she work on a "per project" basis?

> What will the retainer or fee entitle you to? Will submissions cost extra? Does she charge fees for having your work messengered

to the production entity? Does she charge for making copies of your script? What percentage does she charge if she submits your screenplay and it sells?

> Does she become involved in "packaging" a project? That is, will she take your project to the agencies to find either acting or directing talent that will sign on as part of your project? Does she charge extra for doing packaging?

> Is she a member of the California Bar Association (licensed to practice law in the state of California where a majority of the entertainment industry operates)?

> Does she represent other members of the entertainment community besides other writers?

Many agents have strong ties to seasoned entertainment attorneys and many of them work hand-in-hand to represent writers as a team. Most successful writers have both an agent and an entertainment lawyer.

What is an "entertainment manager"?

Entertainment managers are not entirely new to the industry, but there seem to be more managers than ever before. Many well-known former agents (some from the mega-agencies) have set up house as entertainment managers, some of whom will only take on writing clients who are already established.

Like the entertainment attorneys, the managers are not WGA-affiliated. As of this writing, there are no boundaries that regulate a manager, although legally, managers are not allowed to procure work for a client. So when it is time for a writer to have his work shopped around, most managers will usually work in conjunction with an entertainment attorney (who takes 5%) and/or perhaps an agent (who also takes 10%). Entertainment managers can often charge a higher percentage than agents, ranging from the standard 10% to as much as 20% of a writer's gross earnings.

What are the advantages of having a manager? Because managers usually have fewer clients than would an agent, they can often invest more time in helping to mold a writer's career. Several managers are former studio or production execs who act as sounding boards and specialize in helping writers to develop their projects so that they will be "market-ready." Agents (especially ones at the mega-agencies) usually do not have the time to make this kind of effort. Most managers also work as a team with clients who have agents and/or entertainment attorneys, especially when it comes to submissions, negotiations, and packaging.

Also, many managers who take an active interest in their writers may also want to attach themselves as producers if a client's screenplay is sold. Depending on your relationship with your manager and his industry background, such an attachment can often be a blessing or, on rare occasions, a curse.

What is the difference between an agent and an entertainment manager?

By the very nature of the business today, agents seem to be more focused on the bottom line; that is, getting the most money and the best deal for their client. Managers focus more on helping writers to develop their skill set, teaching them about the business side of their craft and guiding them in their career. As one manager astutely put it, "A manager is more about a long-term business plan and keeping a client on track, while an agent is about finding the client the best opportunities today."

What do managers look for in a client?

Managers are looking for clients who are excited about the business, but are realistic at the same time. Having a client with genuine talent is a given, but nowadays, screenwriters also have to be charismatic when they are in meetings — they have to be articulate about their ideas. Writers who are uncomfortable in a room can often be their own worst enemy.

Because The Biz thrives on networking, managers feel it is imperative that writers be collaborative. Those clients who earn a reputation for being hard to work with can quickly fall out of favor and may find it difficult to sell their work or land assignments.

Managers want clients who are dedicated to their writing — who always have lots of ideas, and, most importantly, who follow through on those ideas and are passionate about their craft.

Do I need an entertainment manager?

If you are an emerging writer, having an entertainment manager can be very helpful. Some managers are willing to take on new writers, especially those who have written more than a couple of scripts, even if they do not have produced credits. Entertainment managers will actively help writers to find an agent. Many career scriptwriters have managers and agents, as well as entertainment attorneys.

What is a "script consultant"?

Where do you turn if you have finished your screenplay but would like a professional opinion of the writing quality or marketability before sending your project to an agent, studio or producer? Where can you get an expert's advice on marketing yourself and your work? The answer could be: from a "scriptbuster," otherwise known as a **script consultant.**

Scriptwriting and entertainment consultants were a rarity fifteen to twenty years ago, but in the past decade, a large number of these consultants have emerged. For new scriptwriters, the idea of entrusting their work to the scrutiny of a consultant can be intimidating and daunting, but it can also be extremely time-worthy and cost-effective.

Consultants come in all varieties. Some specialize in helping scriptwriters fine-tune their actual writing skills, while others emphasize an overall professional evaluation of a writer's work. Others concentrate on strategies for marketing a writer and his or her work.

Consultants can serve an important function for emerging scriptwriters — whether Hollywood is in their backyard or not. Most new writers do not have immediate access to networking and to direct communication with others active in the motion picture and television industry. Good consultants should know what is selling and who is looking for what.

At the same time, it is imperative for writers to understand that with such a large volume of material being submitted, a less experienced writer may have only one shot at each studio, production house or agency. Few agents, producers or executives will agree to take a second look at a screenplay, even if the project has been completely revamped and revised. As a result, many scriptwriters want the assurance that each time their work is submitted, it is in the best professional shape possible. Having a consultant look over a writer's work is often the best way to obtain such peace of mind.

Finding a consultant.

One way to find a script consultant is through your writers group or by personal recommendation. Talk with members in your group or with other writers who may have had the opportunity to use or hear about a screenplay specialist, and do not be afraid to query people about their experiences.

Larger literary organizations are also excellent resources for locating individuals who can give you a professional appraisal. Organizations like Scriptwriters Network, Wisconsin Screenwriters Forum or Northwest Screenwriters Guild have listings of consultants who specialize in evaluating film and television projects. A careful search of such writer-friendly magazines and newsletters as *Writer's Digest, The Hollywood Scriptwriter* or *Scr(i)pt* may turn up ads or articles on industry consultants.

Online writers chat groups can often yield other writers who have had the opportunity of hiring a scriptbuster. Word of warning: There have been a number of "consultants" who have advertised online with very low fees who are not legitimate experts. It is always advisable to check out their career background and to ask questions: How long have they been in business? Where did they train, and with whom? You might also ask for references.

If you are attending a writers' conference, you might want to ask some of your fellow participants if they have worked with a competent script specialist. This is not only a great way to obtain the name of an expert, but is also a terrific way to start a networking conversation.

Coverage vs. Consultation

I am often asked if getting "coverage" is the same thing as getting a "consultation."

In the industry, **coverage** refers to the report that a story analyst or reader gives to a screenplay, teleplay, treatment or project proposal that is submitted to a studio, production company or agency. The coverage is usually on a pre-printed form and includes a synopsis of the project and a short overall commentary on the quality of the writing and the submission's commercial potential. Studio and agency coverage forms usually have box scores where the reader or analyst can give a rating from "excellent" all the way down to "poor" on various elements like structure, characters, dialogue, etc.

A **consultation**, on the other hand, is a set of detailed notes on a screenplay, teleplay, treatment or project proposal that is evaluated by a consultant for a writer. There is no synopsis of the plot, nor is there a short overall commentary or box scores. The detailed notes of a consultation will focus on the problem areas of the material and will usually give suggestions on possible solutions as well as guidelines for how a writer should approach the next rewrite.

If a writer wants to know how their script might be evaluated by a reader, there are websites that feature coverage services. What can be somewhat frustrating with most of the online coverage services is that writers usually do not know anything about the person who is reading and critiquing their material, and since the writer already knows his storyline, a synopsis is not really needed and the commentary may not be very specific.

If a writer is interested in getting an in-depth evaluation of his screenplay with specific details, as well as suggestions and guidelines to help with the next revision, then a consultation is probably a better choice. Script consultants usually work individually and not for a "service." Also, it is much easier for a writer to find out more information about the background of an individual script consultant.

Selecting a consultant.

The smart writer will immediately ascertain the credentials of any specialist. How much industry experience does the consultant have, and how current is her connection to film or television? In what capacity has this person worked in the industry (executive, story analyst, writer, producer, acquisitions specialist, agent)? Does the consultant have experience in a specific area that applies to your project (film, television, animation, etc.)?

Has this person taught before? While the consultant you select does not have to be a certified teacher or professor, it is often reassuring to know that the expert has experience in successfully communicating comments, ideas and advice. Teaching experience can include workshops, seminars and conferences.

In addition to asking for industry experience, it is important to find out what critique method is used. How detailed is the critique? Is it verbal (via a phone meeting, personal meeting or by audio cassette)? Is the evaluation a written one? Does the consultant make notations directly into the margins of the script? Is it a combination of any of the above?

Another important and expensive consideration is the consultant's fee. A recent query into current fees for written critiques for full-length motion picture scripts turned up amounts ranging anywhere from $250 for a two-page evaluation, $500 for a five-page critique with script notations, to a whopping $5,000 for a two-page commentary/ letter. Fees also vary according to the length of the material and its type — treatment, television series proposal, story outline or synopsis, feature-length film, half-hour sitcom episode or one-hour dramatic episode. Generally speaking, the lengthier the material, the higher the fee. Some consultants also specialize in reading and evaluating novels with filmic potential in mind, and will give suggestions on how a novel could be best adapted. Fees for this type of consultation are usually "per page."

In rare cases, some screenplay specialists charge by the hour. These fees range from $25 to $250 per hour, often with a two-hour minimum.

Incidentally, most script consultants will not recommend a client's work to an agent or producer unless the story and the writing are extraordinary. Unless a consultant tells you that they would like to personally show your work to a producer, studio or agent, do not assume that the consultant evaluating your project is willing to use industry connections to obtain an agent for you or seek a possible sale for your work.

Knowing what to expect.

If your consultant provides a verbal critique, you can expect a verbal evaluation that lasts anywhere between thirty to sixty minutes in length.

Written evaluations can run from two to five single-spaced pages of commentary, although most consultants seem to average between four to ten pages. Most of the comments are organized in either chronological script order (notes starting with page one and progressing in chronological order to the finish) or by major subject headings (characterization, dialogue, structure, theme, pacing, etc.).

Some consultants will make notations directly on the margins of your screenplay, thus highlighting awkward scene transitions, typos, inconsistent dialogue, pacing problems, questions of logic, etc. Many consultants combine their margin notes with either a written or verbal evaluation so a writer can readily identify the areas of concern discussed in the body of the evaluation.

Most script specialists (but not all) will also include a follow-up. Follow-ups usually take one of two forms:

> A letter written asking any questions the writer may have about the critique.

> A fifteen- to thirty-minute phone call from the writer to discuss any questions the writer may have after reading the evaluation.

Evaluations can be done in as short a time as a few days or as long as four to six weeks, depending upon how detailed an evaluation is requested. Industry consultants usually charge a higher rate if a rush is requested. Ask up front what the consultant's schedule is like. Do not wait until the last week if your goal is to submit your material to meet the deadline of a script competition or fellowship program. If, however, you are up against a time limitation, you will need to decide whether you want to pay the extra money to procure the rush services of a consultant.

Be aware that most industry specialists have other work commitments that may sometimes take precedence over a consultation (unless they are full-time consultants). On the average, it should take anywhere from two to four weeks to get a detailed, five-page evaluation of a feature script. Evaluations of treatments, outlines or shorter pieces of work will probably take slightly less time.

Sending your script.

When sending out your script to a consultant, remember to do the following:

> Send a clean copy (not the original!) of your material. No hand-written notes or corrections, please.

> Be sure your script is on white bond, three-hole punched, and held together with brads that are long enough to secure your work. Card stock covers are optional, but highly recommended. Refer to pages 80–81 for more information.

> All pages should be numbered and in correct sequential order. Check for any missing or duplicate pages.

> Include a cover letter that states what the material is for (a treatment for a Movie-of-the-Week, a proposal for a sitcom, a screenplay for an animated feature film, etc.) and what the genre is (romantic comedy, suspense, action-adventure, horror, etc.). If there are specific questions or areas of concern you would like covered, be sure to mention them in your letter. It is also helpful to let the consultant know if you are planning to submit your work to an agent, producer, or competition.

> While this is purely optional, you might want to include a sentence or two on how the project came to be, if you can do that briefly. It is also helpful to let the consultant know if your material is based on a book or a true-life incident.

> Enclose a SASE large enough and with sufficient postage for the return of your work. If there is a time factor involved, make arrangements for a prepaid rush delivery service (FedEx, DHL, Express Mail, or similar services).

> Do not forget to include your check or money order for the agreed-upon fee (unless your consultant happens to have Pay-Pal), along with your phone number and email address in case the consultant needs to ask you a question or has a scheduling delay.

Reading your evaluation.

Once your material has been evaluated and returned, carefully read (and/or listen to) all the comments, suggestions and margin notes. Then wait a day and read the evaluation again, making notations if there are areas or comments you do not agree with or understand. It is also helpful to note internally why you disagree with the consultant on a specific point. If your evaluation includes a follow-up, list your questions and comments in the order of importance, keeping any limitations in mind (e.g., a written follow-up letter should be no longer than one to one-and-one-half pages, and a follow-up phone call should not exceed the agreed-upon time limit).

Any and all comments made about formatting, typos and misspellings should be heeded and corrected. While the content of your material is the primary focus, any indication that a writer is sloppy or less than professional can sometimes detract from the story you are trying to tell.

If your follow-up is via telephone, carefully make notes on any suggestions or advice the consultant may give. If there is time, you may want to pitch your revision to the consultant for his feedback. This is an excellent way to know if you are on the right track. After your follow-up, sit down with your calendar and make a schedule for your revision, giving yourself a realistic deadline.

Understand up front that you are paying a consultant to give you her unsolicited, unbiased evaluation. You are not paying a consultant to praise your work to the skies unless it truly warrants that praise.

Other helpful consultants.

In addition to consultants who can do an in-depth evaluation of your work, there are other consultants or experts who may also prove helpful to a screenwriter in related areas.

If doing detailed research is not one of your strong suits, or if time is a constraint, you may want to look into the services of a consultant to do your research. Most consultants in this area have an hourly rate, although some will occasionally charge a slightly discounted day rate or "per project" rate.

There are also consultants who will specialize in teaching writers on how to go about marketing themselves and their screenplays. They can assist you in such tasks as narrowing down the best production companies to approach about your project or helping you to write a selling synopsis, or their specialty might be acting as a screenwriter's pitching coach.

Another service that a scriptwriter may need is someone who specializes in the area of career consulting. There are also therapists who focus on the psychological aspects of screenwriting — such as writer's block, dealing with rejection, or facing the fear of public speaking.

As is the case in locating and selecting the services of a script consultant, it is always best to ask for opinions or personal recommendations from peers in writers groups, scriptwriting chat rooms, or when networking at conferences or pitchfests.

What agents, attorneys, managers, and consultants cannot do.

While agents, attorneys, managers and consultants can help a writer by submitting your work, negotiating your contract, and giving you a professional evaluation, your greatest ally is yourself. Agents, attorneys, managers and consultants cannot guarantee you work, nor can they guarantee you a career. They are professionals who can help facilitate your career.

The most successful writers in the industry did not get to the top by laying back and having their cadre of agents, managers and attorneys do their job. It is imperative that writers realize that in this business, you have to keep on top of things. Continue to network and research by bringing any interesting project-related information to the attention of your agent or manager. If you happen to meet a production exec at a party and he or she expresses an interest in seeing your work, set up a meeting yourself and tell your agent or manager about it. By letting your agent and/or manager know what you are doing, you will assure that you are not stepping on his toes. It could be that your agent is working on getting a meeting for you with another exec at that company.

As in any other business, open communication is the key to gaining information that will help you to get ahead and forge better working relationships.

Protecting your work.

In addition to registering your screenplay with the Writers Guild of America, you should also consider the following advice given to me by several of my writer friends:

Copies.

Always have extra copies of your work, either paper copies or computer files saved on discs. In general, backup discs are the best choice. If you do not have access to a computer or are computer-shy, consider having a computer-literate friend or relative enter your material onto disc. In addition, there are service bureaus that do disc conversions and scanning for a fee.

Never send the original of your work to anyone — send a copy only. It is amazing how many new writers will send me the original of their work. While most executives, producers, agents and consultants are honest and reliable, it is still best to send only a copy.

Be sure your copies include all pages and that all copies are clean and legible. There is nothing more frustrating than reading a script that has missing pages. And third- or fourth-generation copies can strain the eyes (and patience) of anyone evaluating your material.

Storage.

Invest in a fire-rated document filing box or a safety deposit box. Keep original paper copies and backup discs stored in these boxes. Fire-rated document boxes can be pricey, but they are worth the cost to ensure one's peace of mind. For a nominal fee, you can rent a safety deposit box at your local bank. Check first; these boxes are not always large enough to accommodate full-length screenplays, but can usually accommodate discs.

In addition, keep a backup disc or flash drive with a trusted friend or relative. One writer told me that he sends a disc of each completed script to his sister, who lives out of state. Some have told him that this is a bit of an over-reaction on his part, but he claims the ground never shakes in his hometown in Iowa, and he still does not trust living on Southern California soil.

These precautions so far have addressed the physical protection of your treatments, teleplays and screenplays. But you also need to take precautions that address the possibility of fraud, theft or plagiarism. Remember, however, that you are protecting only your particular collection of words, not the overall idea. In fact, it has been my experience that great ideas (as opposed to actual scripts or books) are not exclusive to any one person. Given the large number of treatments and scripts submitted every year, there are relatively few valid cases of theft or plagiarism that come to court. However, all writers are wise to consider the following protection.

Release forms.

If you do not have an agent, it is imperative that you sign a release form whenever you submit a project. Simply ask the production company or agency for a release form. If the company does not provide one, send your own. Most scriptwriters' groups have access to copies of standard release forms. Also, InkTip has an industry standard release form on their website (*inktip.com*).

While these forms provide few guarantees (except for title of work and date of submission), they can serve as additional proof if you find yourself in a legal hassle with the company or agency. Writers, especially those trying to get their first break, should keep in mind that the production company and/or agency is doing them a favor by considering their material. Once you have an agent and/or have more industry experience under your belt, release forms will become unnecessary.

Paper trail.

Consider starting a file for each project. List the date and time of each meeting (whether in person or in an extended conference call) where you discuss or pitch one of your projects. Under each listing, note the following:

> Did you leave a copy of the script or treatment or a pitch on paper?

> If so, which version?

> Who was in attendance at the meeting?

> Did anyone take notes?

> What was their reaction to the pitch?

You may want to send a note to the executive or producer, thanking him or her for the chance to discuss your project. This is not only common courtesy and a valuable part of networking, but it also leaves a paper trail that can refresh your memory, should it become necessary in an arbitration. Be sure to put a copy of any correspondence concerning one of your projects into your project file. One writer uses separate flash drives for records on each of her projects and another scripter uses individual discs for his records.

If you have an agent or manager, call shortly after the pitch or meeting. Let your agent or manager know how the meeting went. Note which project(s) you pitched or discussed and what the exec's or producer's reaction or attitude was. This is part of communicating with your agent and will give her an idea of how best to follow up with the exec or producer.

While agents usually keep a written phone log and notations on their clients' meetings, most writers tell me that they also keep their own project meeting files. They do this in case they ever find it necessary to change agencies or their agent moves on to another firm or a non-agent position.

With good fortune, hopefully none of you will ever experience the loss of your work to a natural disaster or an unscrupulous person. But taking some preventive measures in advance can go a long way toward keeping any disaster from also including your work.

Chapter 14

The Animation Revolution: So Much More Than Saturday Morning Cartoons

Part of my job as an exec at Disney TV Animation included dropping in on voice recording sessions from time to time. It was Friday and we were behind schedule and needed to ship out the script, storyboard material and the voice recording to our overseas animation house for one of our episodes that night. It was during one of those Asian flu epidemics and two of our voiceover actors got sick, which meant the remaining two who were there were doing double duty. The last scene had been recorded and the actors had left for the weekend. As the producer and I were getting ready to call it a day, one of the recording engineers ran into the room. In playing back the last few scenes, he realized one of the microphones must have malfunctioned. The producer let out a string of un-Disneylike words — he clearly didn't want to wait until Monday to re-record a few youngsters' "yelps and screams." All of a sudden the recording engineer whispered in the producer's ear and they both looked at me. The producer asked, "You wouldn't happen to want to do us all a favor and save us a ton of money, would you?" The next thing I knew, I was in front of a microphone with a headset on and I was screaming and yelping my head off, pretending that I was in the backseat of an out-of-control car going down a winding mountain road!

Little did the producer realize that he had just done me a favor by fulfilling one of my dreams!

Once considered the little-mentioned stepchild of moviemaking, animation has exploded in the last ten years, giving screenwriters, directors, actors and producers another lucrative filmmaking outlet.

Animation is now considered big business — so much so, that many of the major motion picture studios in the U.S. have established an animation division or have joined forces with a partner company. With the advancement and acceptance of high technology, an animated film no longer has to take three to five years to make. And with the heightened interest in animation, more colleges and universities are teaching the skills necessary to produce animated projects.

Technology has also spread globally, which has helped countries around the world to develop and achieve the artistic and technological skills necessary to open up animation houses. Countries like Singapore, Thailand, Japan, the Philippines, India, Taiwan, Ireland, as well as several countries in South America, are now sharing in the financial jackpot of animated projects. With a larger talent pool around the world, countries can vie for business, oftentimes at far more competitive rates than in North America and Western Europe.

Animation is not only for theatrical movies, cartoons and television series — animation can now be found in promotions, advertising, and as active "titles" instead of boring credits of block letters against a solid color screen. Animation is also used in music videos, and there are dozens of animated shorts and Web series on the Internet. Sophisticated styles of computerized animation are used in conjunction with live-action movies (think *Avatar, Polar Express, 300, Alice In Wonderland*). Some of the writers, directors and producers of the most popular animated films got their start doing commercials, credits, or doing computerized animation sequences in live-action films before getting their big break doing animated television series or working for theatrical animation powerhouses like Pixar or DreamWorks Animation.

With the popularity of such successful projects as the *Toy Story* franchise, *Monsters Inc., Happy Feet,* and *The Incredibles*, animated movies now have a category of their own on Oscar night! And top-named celebs — many of who are now parents — eagerly sign up to be "voice personalities" for animated projects. Celebrities like Cameron Diaz, Mike Myers, Eddie Murphy, Julia Roberts, Meg Ryan, Bruce Willis,

Tom Hanks, Jerry Seinfeld, Renée Zellweger, Penélope Cruz, Woody Allen, Miley Cyrus, and dozens of other "big names" have added their recognizable voices and acting talent to some of the most successful animated films. Popular singers, songwriters and musicians are also composing musical scores and theme songs for animated projects, which also help to boost additional revenues.

And as if all of the above were not enough, projects that were once comic books, cartoons and animated movies are being franchised into live-action movies, ice shows, video games and Broadway musicals. For animation writers, if you create characters for an animated TV series or movie which becomes very successful, there is now the added possibility of seeing those characters crossing over to other forms of media and revenue that goes beyond the usual stuffed animals, books, action figures and games for Nintendo and PlayStation.

Historically, most animated features were usually dependent on comic book heroes or familiar fairy tale characters for their market-ability. But thanks to a general overall acceptance of animation as a more serious storytelling device, and the emergence of technology that shortens the production time and budget, writing for animation is no longer reliant on familiar childhood stories or superheroes.

What makes writing for animation different than writing for live-action?

Whereas most animated projects in the past relied more heavily on lots of physical gags with very simple and familiar storylines, animated features of today are more sophisticated, with more attention paid to character development and dialogue than ever before.

Pacing is usually much faster, and most animated movies — especially those aimed for the younger market — are slightly shorter in length than the average live-action project. But there are also some very successful animated films which had screenplays that crossed over the 100-page mark, such as *Ratatouille*, *Up*, and *Shrek*.

Sound effects and the inclusion of musical scores are encouraged in many of the animated films. Animated films from Pixar and Dream-Works, in particular, almost always have a well-known songwriting and composing team that works closely with the screenwriter and artists once a script has been purchased or optioned and throughout the entire development and storyboarding process. And while physical humor and gags are still a mainstay, many of the latest animated films now include "sight" gags, puns, popular cultural references and more sophisticated humor, all of which appeals to a much wider audience age range.

Animated writers are expected to always think more visually and imaginatively. When writing about the "world" in which your story takes place, think of that world as an actual character. Your narrative description should give us a sense of the pace, time period, location, and geographical and cultural oddities that will serve as a backdrop for your characters and their story. Is it in the sewers of a large, bustling city? A small, rural village back in the Middle Ages? Deep in a rainforest amidst the ruins of an abandoned Asian civilization? Or on a parched, desolate planet where aliens have to live in sandstone caverns?

Think fun.

Although some animated movies and TV series are more dramatic in content, it is important to remember that a large share of the animated audience is children. This means it is important to "think fun" by not only tapping into the creative imagination and fantasy of the "child within us," but infusing the characters and/or the situation with a sense of humor and fun. Humor can take many forms — slapstick, exaggerated caricatures or personalities (think Cruella De Vil of *101 Dalmations*), the nonsensical, sight and sound gags, to name a few.

More than anything else, you will notice that contemporary animated movies and television series have various levels of humor that appeal to both younger members of the audience as well as to adults. Examples of such dual-focused humor can be found in such animated projects as the popular *Shrek* and *Ice Age* franchises, *The Simpsons* and *Madagascar*.

Think genre.

While superheroes, legends and storybook fairy tales started out as the mainstay of animated fare, writers are encouraged to "think genre." Of the fifty highest-grossing motion pictures, you will find several animated films. Here are some examples of popular genres for animated movies:

Comedy — *Over The Hedge, Ratatouille, Happy Feet, Toy Story.*

Action-Adventure — *Aladdin, Tarzan, Up, The Jungle Book.*

Drama — *Mulan, The Lion King.*

Mystery/Supernatural — *Spirited Away, Howl's Moving Castle.*

Fairy Tales & Legends — *The Little Mermaid, The Princess And The Frog, Hercules.*

Animal Antics — *Babar, Ice Age, A Bug's Life, Antz, Madagascar, Finding Nemo.*

Think family.

It may surprise you that children do not have to always take center stage in an animated storyline, even though they often comprise a majority of your target demographic. In looking over some of the more popular family films, it is interesting to note that the primary motor driving these films is seeing adults or teens in funny, outrageous and/or out-of-control situations. In *Cloudy With A Chance Of Meatballs*, most of the fairy tale-based films (*Snow White, Sleeping Beauty, Cinderella*), and such successful favorites as *Wall-E, Madagascar, Happy Feet*, and *Shrek*, you will notice that these films do not rely on children as the main characters and frequently do not even feature human characters. Instead, the story is populated with animals or normally inanimate objects that have the ability to talk, react and think like humans, which adds an imaginative and humorous level of entertainment.

Animated films of the past were mostly targeting children under ten years of age. Today, studios are looking for animated projects that can appeal to a family. This means they want projects with "crossover appeal" that will attract not only children, but also older siblings, teens and adults.

Thinking "family" is a smart move — after all, it is usually the parents, older siblings, babysitters or grandparents who accompany children to the theater and usually determine what movies will be seen. Thus, it is important that the main thrust of the movie appeals to as wide a range of audience demographics as possible. If your project can appeal to the "child" in most adults, you will likely have a project that will ultimately attract the entire family.

When thinking "family," the cardinal rule is to suppress the urge to write "down" to a child's level. Most young people today understand much more than we give them credit for, and as soon as their attention waivers, they will outspokenly label a TV show or movie as "babyish" and will quickly lose interest.

The Incredibles, Ratatouille, The Nightmare Before Christmas, and *Up* are excellent examples of animated projects that appealed to a larger audience range and not just to children.

Tips for animation writers.

I recently moderated a panel with several animation writers and here are some of their tips and advice for writers who are specifically tackling an animated project.

Be sure that you have a consistent "tone" in your animated project, whether it is an animated TV series or a feature film. Here are some examples:

> **Physical Comedy** — *Animaniacs, Cloudy With A Chance of Meatballs.*

> **Edgy** — *South Park, Beavis & Butthead, The Nightmare Before Christmas.*

> **Sitcom** — *The Simpsons, King of the Hill, Rugrats.*

> **Edu-tainment** — *Dora The Explorer, Ni Hao Kai-Lan, Ready Set Learn.*

> **Story/Fable** — *Aladdin, The Little Mermaid, Lilo & Stitch.*

> **Action-Adventure** — *Transformers: Generation 2, Star Wars: Clone Wars.*

When writing for an animated TV series or film, be aware of the standard "length" of each episode/special:

> Five- to six-minute shorts

> Ten-minute episodic (two for each thirty-minute time slot)

> Twenty-two-minute episodic (usually one per thirty-minute time slot)

> Twenty-two-minute special (one per thirty-minute time slot)

> Forty-five-minute special or made for DVD (one per sixty-minute time slot)

> Seventy- to ninety-minute theatrical animated film

In creating an animated main character for a TV series, take the following into consideration:

> Someone/something that kids (or the "child in all of us") can readily relate to — say, a group of animals at the zoo want to see what life is like on the other side of the walls (*Madagascar*) — appeals to kids who are curious about what lies beyond the familiarity of their home.

> Quirks, flaws, personality traits (both good and bad) that are not only relatable, but can be used to promote the storyline and keep the audience engaged — for instance, a Donkey who talks incessantly when he's nervous and insecure, but is the most loyal friend an ogre could ever have. (*Shrek*)

> Consistency of personality range and sense of humor.

> Conflict/contrast between character personalities — e.g., in *The Little Mermaid*, Sebastian is older and wiser, in sharp and entertaining contrast to Ariel's other friend, Flounder, who is young and free-spirited, with a curiosity that often gets him in trouble.

Here are four important things to keep in mind when creating a main character for an animated movie:

1. A clearly defined need or goal. In most instances, the main character's initial need or goal may change as the story progresses and another need or goal will take on more significance.

EXAMPLES:

In *Mulan*, Mulan's goal is to take her disabled father's place in the Emperor's army in the fight against the invading Huns.

In *Shrek*, Shrek's goal is to take back his beloved swamp home.

2. A strong conflict involved in meeting that initial need or achieving that initial goal.

EXAMPLES:

In *Mulan*, Mulan's identity as a female in the army must not be discovered or she and her family could face death.

In *Shrek*, Shrek agrees to rescue a princess for Lord Farquaad in exchange for the reclaiming of his swamp.

3. A plan of action.

EXAMPLES:

In *Mulan*, Mulan's plan is to prove her abilities as a soldier to save her fellow troops and her country.

In *Shrek*, after he rescues Fiona, Shrek must escape the dragon's lair and fight his conflicting feelings for Fiona.

4. A resolution to both the inner and outer conflict the character feels.

EXAMPLES:

In *Mulan*, Mulan saves her country, comes to terms with her attraction to Shang, and proves to all that the worth of a woman is not in an arranged marriage, but in her value as an individual.

In *Shrek*, Shrek takes back his swampland home, saves the fairy tale folks from Farquaad's wrath, and comes to terms with his need for love and friendship, thanks to Fiona and Donkey.

Writing a log line or springboard for your animated project.

As with a live-action project, a writer will be expected to have a log line for an animated project. Sometimes the term **springboard** will be used instead of log line, but the two terms mean the same thing: a one- or two-sentence summation of your animated film or episode for an animated series.

Just as we did for a live-action film, we start off with a simple statement and build upon it. Let's use *Shrek* as an example:

Ogre rescues Princess.

Lonely Ogre rescues a beautiful Princess for an evil Lord.

Lonely Ogre falls in love with a beautiful Princess he has rescued for an evil Lord.

With a talkative Donkey in tow, a lonely Ogre falls in love with a beautiful Princess he has rescued for an evil Lord.

With the help of a talkative Donkey, a reclusive Ogre falls in love with a beautiful Princess he has rescued for an evil Lord, only to learn she harbors a dark secret that may keep them apart.

Writing a premise for your animated project.

A **premise** for a possible episode on an animated series or for an animated theatrical film is essentially constructed like a P.O.P. for a live-action film.

Using *Shrek* as an example, here is a one-page premise for an animated movie:

Shrek — Premise.

Once upon a time in a far-away swamp, there lived an ornery green ogre named SHREK whose lonely existence is suddenly shattered when a wisecracking DONKEY — running for his life — ends up at Shrek's doorstep. Intending to let the persistent Donkey stay for only one night, Shrek awakens to find his swamp has been overrun by dozens of annoying fairytale characters. There are BLIND MICE in his food, a BIG BAD WOLF in his bed, THREE LITTLE PIGS and more — all banished from their kingdom by the evil LORD FARQUAAD, whose one desire is to marry a princess and become a king.

Determined to help these banished characters and to keep his beloved swamp, Shrek cuts a deal with the height-challenged Farquaad and sets out to rescue the beautiful PRINCESS FIONA so that Farquaad can become king and Shrek can go back to his quiet existence. Accompanying Shrek on his mission, Donkey claims he'll do anything for Shrek — except shut up. Rescuing Fiona from a fiery DRAGON or Farquaad and his over-zealous Soldiers may prove to be the least of their problems when Shrek finds himself falling for Fiona and realizes she's hiding a deep, dark secret.

Will Shrek finally admit his love for Fiona? Will Farquaad marry the Princess and become king? Will the banished fairy tale characters ever leave the swamp? And will Donkey ever shut up?

If you are writing a premise for a spec episode for an animated television series, here is an example of a premise, kindly supplied for us by screenwriter Marlowe Weisman for the *Aladdin* TV series:

Aladdin, *"Some Enchanted Genie"* — Episodic Premise.

GENIE is forced to sleep in a smelly shoe after power-hungry wizard ABIS MAL and HAROUD steal his lamp. When Genie, ALADDIN, IAGO, ABU and CARPET pursue them to the romantic city of PARRAH-MOOR, Genie falls head over tail for EDEN, a female Genie of the Bottle. Finding the lamp empty, Mal steals Eden's bottle from her little orphan master DHANDI. Just as the two genies hit it off on their first date, Eden is summoned away to serve her new evil master, leaving an unknowing Genie heartbroken. Mal forces a reluctant Eden to banish Genie to the ocean depths, then wishes himself into an all-powerful COSMIC, CLOUD-LIKE BEING. As Mal tries to get the hang of his thunderous new powers (with humorous results), Eden has left Genie an escape! Genie flies to rescue Aladdin and Eden while taking the wind out of the wizard's cloud. Bittersweet finale as Genie begs Eden to run away with him and she chooses to stay with Dhandi instead — the child needs her. The genies part, but not before making a date to reunite in the distant future.

Types of animated projects.

Animation projects come in all lengths and formats. You will note that there are some odd numbers given for the length of the written material. Although thirty minutes is how long each series episode lasts, writers have to remember that commercials and opening and closing credits will take up some time as well.

If you are fortunate enough to be able to pitch a spec episode, you should be prepared with a log line/springboard and at least a one- to one-and-one-half-page premise. Animation writers often arm themselves with at least one or two additional spec episode ideas as added insurance.

Animated Shorts — Shorts are generally referred to as the original cartoons. They are the shortest in length, usually between four to six minutes. There are no act breaks. The original *Looney Tunes* shorts are probably the best examples of this type of project — very little dialogue, mostly a series of chases and physical gags. Think *Tom & Jerry*, *Porky Pig*, *Bugs Bunny*, *Daffy Duck*. Premises for a spec animated short are usually one-half to one page and scripts are usually between nine to twelve pages. Many students specializing in animation will produce at least one or two shorts as part of their graduating portfolio, which is then used as work samples when approaching animation houses and producers for work. Pixar often produces shorts to run before some of their feature-length films in theaters and on DVDs.

Ten-Minute Animated TV Episode — Some animated television series (usually the ones for younger audiences under five years) will have two stories per half-hour show to accommodate the shorter attention spans for the preschool audience. Think *Winnie The Pooh* or *Tiny Toons*. There is slightly more dialogue, but very simple storylines. An episode can be mostly gags, although *Winnie The Pooh* is known for fewer gags and more emphasis on problem-solving issues like sharing, caring, being a good friend, etc. Each episode is approximately ten to eleven minutes in length, with one act break, with the first part being six or seven minutes in length and the second part being three to four minutes long. Premises for a spec animated ten-minute episode are from one to one-and-one-half pages and scripts are usually between sixteen and eighteen pages in length.

Twenty-Two-Minute Animated TV Episode — A twenty-two-minute episode for a half-hour animated TV series is a single episode. *Dora The Explorer* and *Busytown Mysteries* are two examples of an animated single-story episode. There is usually a main ("A") story and a secondary ("B") story. There is much more emphasis on dialogue and plots are not as simplistic as shorts or ten-minute episodics. With *Dora*, there is an educational component that usually focuses on learning geography and short Spanish phrases. With *Busytown*, there is at least one major mystery to be solved. There are usually three act breaks with the first being slightly longer at eight to ten minutes in length, the second being seven to nine minutes, and the last being five to seven minutes. Premises for a spec animated twenty-two-minute episode range from one to one-and-one-half pages and scripts are usually between thirty-six and forty-two pages long.

Animated TV Special/DVD — With a half-hour special (e.g., *A Charlie Brown Christmas*), there are usually two or three act breaks and you can follow the format for a twenty-two-minute TV episodic format above. If it is for a one-hour TV special, you will be writing to fill forty-five minutes, which means there may be five or six act breaks. If it is for an animated DVD, there will be no act breaks. Occasionally, more popular animated TV specials (especially the ones for young children and the ones that have been holiday specials) will be released on DVD without act breaks in the middle, or you might be given an assignment to create a direct-to-DVD animated special utilizing already established characters focusing on a holiday or specific theme. Half-hour special premises are one to one-and-one-half pages in length and one-hour specials are one-and-one-half to two pages long. Half-hour special scripts are the same as twenty-two-minute episodes and one-hour special scripts are from fifty to fifty-eight pages long.

Animated Theatrical/Feature Film — Most animated films run anywhere from seventy to ninety minutes in length, although by the time all the beginning and end credits are added on, they occasionally run over 100 minutes. Screenplays for animated feature films can run anywhere from as little as seventy-five pages to more than 100 pages. If you have an animated theatrical project, you should be prepared with a log line or elevator pitch, a one-page P.O.P., and a two- to three-page selling synopsis, just as you would for a live-action motion picture.

Animation reality check.

Although animation has become the new darling in filmmaking, be aware that there are hundreds of animated projects submitted each year to producers of the animated format — in fact, thousands of projects are likely submitted to well-known animation venues like Warner Bros., Pixar/Disney, and DreamWorks Animation.

Many of the larger animation venues prefer to develop their characters in-house. However, if you have had experience in a related field — commercials, majored in animation in college, worked in a special effects house, have special training in computer graphics, have done assignments (written and/or artistic) for graphic design houses, comic book/anime/manga, etc. — it might be easier for you to submit original material.

Also, if you are willing to put your original material aside, you may want to consider submitting samples of animated television series spec episodes to series producers and head writers, should there be an opening on staff or for a freelance assignment. This is an excellent way to gain more experience in the field and to make valuable contacts before making the leap to creating your own series or film.

Although it is not a must, some writers in the animation field have found it beneficial to pair up with a partner who can bring more of a visual component to the project. It is not unusual for an animation writer to partner with a storyboard artist or a specialist in computer graphics or animated character development. Having a partner who has experience in the visual arena also doubles the contact possibilities for a duo and can actually lend more depth and credence to a project.

However, as mentioned previously, some animation houses are known for having a distinct signature animation style, and having a storyboard, developed character samples and other visuals may not always prove to be a plus when submitting a project. It is important to do your homework and see which animation houses and producers are the best fit for your project.

Here are some questions to ask yourself before querying or submitting your material:

> Does this venue have other produced series or films in the same genre as your project? Having credits in the same genre often means that they prefer projects that are similar.

> Do their projects have a distinct physical style, or does their visual style change according to the genre? If their projects have a more distinct style, it could be a sign that they prefer doing their projects in-house to have a consistency in style and a "signature" look.

> Does your project require a more "realistic" look to the animation? If so, you may want to take a careful look to see if the production company can afford to do this more labor-intensive type of animation — in other words, a smaller animation house whose projects feature a more simplistic style of animation may not be as appropriate a fit as a venue that has done a few projects that have a more detailed, "realistic" look to them.

> Does the venue produce both television and feature animation, or just television or just feature films or just shorts? Unless you know for a fact that the animation house does various forms of animation, target only those companies that produce the same form as your submission (i.e., shorts, series for network/cable TV, feature film, etc.).

> How long has the company been in business? And if they are fairly new, check on the principals of the company — what other places have they worked/trained at? What kinds of animated projects did they work on previously?

Contrary to popular belief, "cartoons" are not easy or simple. And writing in the animation field requires a much keener visual sensibility, an active imagination, and an open mind in combining the literal and the visual with technology.

If you are interested in writing for animation and would like additional information regarding membership, rates, conditions, policies and benefits, there are two unions that animation writers can choose to join.

There is the Animation Writers Caucus, which is part of the Writers Guild of America. They are housed at the same address as the WGA (7000 West Third Street, Los Angeles, CA 90048), but they have their own phone line (323-782-4511) and website (*awn.com/wga*).

In addition to the WGA Animation Writers Caucus, an animation writer may choose to join The Animation Guild, which is part of the International Alliance of Theatrical and Stage Employees Union (IATSE). The Animation Guild is located at 1105 No. Hollywood Way, Burbank, CA 91505; (818) 845-7500; *animationguild.org*.

For more specific details on the animation process, writing an animated motion picture, cartoon or creating/writing for an animation series, I'd like to suggest that you check out the following helpful books:

> *Animation Unleashed* by Ellen Besen

> *Animation Writing And Development: From Script Development to Pitch* by Jean Ann Wright

> *How To Write For Animation* by Jeffrey Scott

> *Writing For Animation And Games* by Christy Marx

Chapter 15

Using The Internet: How The Web Can Be Your New B.F.F.

Writer-director-teacher Scott Rice was kicking back with his friends in Texas, discussing the most common mistakes that unproduced screenwriters always seem to make. Somehow or another it came up that there really ought to be a law about writers making these same mistakes over and over again. Suddenly, the light bulb went off for Scott: Why not do a mockumentary about these mistakes and have cops go after these law-breaking writers? Thus, a series of shorts, entitled Script Cops, was born. Initially shown between movies that were featured at the Austin Film Festival, Scott's shorts soon became the "darling" of the film festival circuit, garnering a number of awards. A Sony exec recognized Scott's talents and before long, Sony was funding more episodes of Script Cops, which became an overnight Internet sensation with well over a million hits and counting.

The Internet has quickly become yet another viable option for screenwriters who are eager to break into the entertainment arena. Legions of both produced and unproduced directors and writers are putting together two- to fifteen-minute "shorts" (anywhere from one to six scenes) or "trailers" (similar to the coming attractions that precede the feature films in movie theaters) of their projects on YouTube, MySpace, Vemio, and other websites. Some of these shorts have caught fire and have actually spurred film and television production companies and agents to sign some of these industrious and creative types.

One interesting observation is that there seems to be a similar ratio of good to bad shorts on the Internet just as there are good to bad screenplays that are submitted to networks, producers and studios. One out of every ten shorts might have some merit. And one out of every ten of those may become successful enough to gain enough traffic to become a Web sensation.

Marketing your project on the Web.

If you do not have a short or trailer to show online, but have at least one screenplay you would like to have noticed, there are also numerous websites devoted to posting log lines, synopses and sometimes even partial or entire scripts for others to read and for potential buyers to seek out. While this is certainly one way to get your work "out there," there is also the danger of having a writer's work exposed and possibly stolen, altered or plagiarized.

The following are a few of the more reputable websites (recommended by clients, colleagues, screenwriting groups, and emerging writers) that feature members' postings of log lines and synopses. The websites also offer free access to a number of producers, studio execs, agents and managers, some of whom have found projects and writers on these sites. These sites include:

InkTip (*inktip.com*)

Hollywood Lit Sales (*hollywoodlitsales.com*)

MovieBytes/ScriptLinks (*moviebytes.com/ws/scriptlinks.cfm*)

There are at least a dozen more websites that have popped up in the last couple of years, some of which may be strong possibilities as well. Here are some things to consider if you are thinking of using a website to market your film or television/cable project:

> Find out as much as you can about the person running the website. If there is an email or phone number, contact the person and ask for his background and a history of the company if none is given on the site.

> What fees are being required for your work to be posted on the website? How long will your work remain on the website? What are other similar websites charging for a fee?

> Is a hard copy or an email of the listed available projects being sent on a regular basis to reliable agents, studio execs and production companies, or are the website creators relying on industry personnel to stumble across their services? In what ways and using what methods are the owners marketing their website to the industry? Can they be found on the most popular search engines like Google, Yahoo!, etc.?

> How long has the site been in business? Can it name some of the production companies, studios and agencies that regularly use the site?

> Does the website have links to other industry-related sites or writing organizations? Generally speaking, the more recognized and legitimate a website is, the more professional links or connections it will have to other film and television sites.

> Does the website have an industry professional who regularly answers questions, writes a column/blog, or is featured online? Again, if an executive, consultant, agent or screenwriter in The Biz is featured, it usually indicates that the site has been checked out by the studio, production company or agency that employs the professional.

> What exactly is required of you, the writer, to have your work put online? Is it a log line of fifty words or less? Is it a three-paragraph or three-page synopsis of your work? Or is it an excerpt of your screenplay or the entire script? Posting a log line or synopsis of your screenplay on a marketing website is pretty common. But I would proceed with caution if you are asked to post an excerpt or the entire script. If your synopsis is well written, it should give the interested agent, producer or exec enough of an idea on whether they would like to take things a step further and request your screenplay.

> What kinds of guarantees can the website give you regarding its security? Most legitimate screenplay marketing websites usually require that your project be registered with the WGA or is copyrighted.

> What kinds of "success stories" can they give you? Does the website regularly mention any of these success stories?

> If you are a member of a large writers group or participate in one of the dozens of screenwriting chat rooms that have been formed online, ask if anyone is familiar with the websites you are considering and/or if anyone has had good or bad experiences utilizing any of them. A "thumbs up" from a couple of other fellow screenwriters is usually a pretty good recommendation, and most peers are usually eager to exchange information like this. It is interesting to note that some screenwriting groups also keep track of any questionable experiences on not only script marketing sites, but negative feedback on poorly-run competitions, consultants they feel did not give them their money's worth, or persons trying to pass themselves off as WGA-affiliated agents.

Consider a screenplay reading.

One of the more recent innovations in getting the work of new screenwriters recognized is TriggerStreet (*triggerstreet.com*), the brainchild of producer Dana Brunetti (*Beyond the Sea*, *21*, *Fanboys*) and

Oscar-winning actor Kevin Spacey. Scriptwriters are encouraged to submit their screenplays and a cadre of volunteer readers will read and assess each script and winnow down the selection to one lucky writer's screenplay each month. The screenplay that is selected will be read and recorded by professional actors.

While well-known actors are usually not involved with this type of reading, TriggerStreet has a large pool of acting talent located all over North America who feel that volunteering to do these readings is also a proactive way to network and to have their acting talent both utilized and recognized. Because the actors are in different cities, they will often use Skype to do their recorded reading, while the director also does his job by remote audio. The recorded reading is then edited and mixed to MP3 for replay and is then posted on the TriggerStreet website, where members (yes, many of whom are industry producers, execs and agents) can listen to the selected screenplays at their leisure — like in the comfort of their Beamer while they are stuck in L.A.'s never-ending traffic jam! Almost everything is done on a volunteer basis, but TriggerStreet's goal is to complete at least one audio reading of an unproduced screenplay each month.

Virtual pitching.

While most scriptwriters will unanimously agree that nothing beats being able to meet and greet agents, producers and execs in person, writers are finding that the next best thing is what the industry refers to as **virtual pitching**. What is so great about virtual pitching is that all you really need is your trusty computer and webcam and to sign up and pay for an online pitch session. Here are three recommended options in the area of virtual pitching:

StoryLink is a writer-based community that grew out of The Writers Store in Los Angeles. StoryLink has a feature called Pitch Perfect (*storylink.com/pitchperfect*) that encourages its members to video their pitches in the comfort of their own home and then upload their pitch and post it onto StoryLink. Writers are then asked to choose the genre and a few select key words they feel best describes their project, such as "teen comedy, female lead, off-beat, low-budget" (which might have been the description for a project like *Juno*) or "adult comedy, male buddy, set in Vegas" (which could aptly describe *The Hangover*). There is a nominal fee per project and fees depend on the length of time you want to post your project, usually anywhere from three months to twelve months.

Also, if you happen to be a member of the WGA and would like to post your latest spec project, or if you are an emerging writer and have just won a screenwriting competition, StoryLink will allow you to post your pitch for free. The staff at The Writers Store is so pro-writer that if you do not have access to a webcam, you are welcome to drop by their store in Burbank (3510 West Magnolia Blvd., Burbank, CA 91505; 800-272-8927) and they will gladly assist you in recording and posting your story pitch.

Producers, agents and industry execs who wish to take advantage of Pitch Perfect must register with StoryLink. Membership for producers, agents and execs is absolutely free once their credentials and references are verified, and they can then log in at any time, 24/7, to view as many pitches as they would like. If they are looking for a specific genre, they can easily locate the pitches that meet their needs by narrowing down their search using key words. The search feature saves the industry pros from having to scroll through a long list of pitches, most of which might not fit in their wish list.

Fade In magazine not only sponsors the long-running Hollywood Pitchfest, but also has an online version where you can actually pitch "live" to agents, managers, execs and producers. Again, all you will really need is your computer and a webcam. *Fade In* limits the number of registrants to 100, so early registration is strongly encouraged. There is a nominal fee for each meeting requested. About ten days prior to the pitchfest, you will be emailed a list of the industry professionals who will be participating in the online event. You will then have the opportunity to select your top ten meetings plus five alternates, and *Fade In* will create an appointment schedule for you, which will be emailed to you twenty-four hours in advance. The schedule will give you the approximate "meeting" times when you will be contacted via live video conferencing by the Industry VIPs you have selected. The meetings are up to ten minutes in length. For additional details on *Fade In*'s next Online Hollywood Pitch Festival, go to their website at *fadeinonline.com/events/hpf-online*.

ScriptCoach has yet another option for writers to "pitch in your pajamas" — those are their exact words! — via VirtualPitchfest. This online service allows you to pitch your query letter, which is then posted for producers, execs, managers and agents to see, with VirtualPitchfest's assurance of a guaranteed response back. Again, there is a nominal fee, but they occasionally have specials which can be cost-saving, especially if you happen to be a prolific screenwriter and have a number of projects. Some of their success stories include competition winners, newly-represented writers, and options of screenplays. For more details, visit their website at *virtualpitchfest.com*.

Writing for the Web.

In addition to using the Internet to market your latest feature film script or your television or cable series, the Web is also an exciting new arena where writers can also create and provide entertainment content. I had the opportunity to discuss Web-writing opportunities and experiences with the following writers, teachers, and writer-directors: Michael Ajakwe, Terry Borst, Carolyn Miller, Scott Rice, and Laurie Scheer.

Writers-authors Terry Borst and Carolyn Miller were quick to point out the amazing range of opportunities that await writers who might be interested in writing for Web content:

> Webisodes (serialized stories told in episodic form, mostly live-action, some animation).

> Shorts (can be of most any genre, both live-action and animation)

> Informational sites (on specialized topics such as health, travel, food, lifestyle, sports, etc.).

> Interactive mystery and adventure stories.

> Various types of narrative-heavy games.

Since most writers who are reading this book have been focusing more specifically on traditional storytelling projects, we will be targeting the webisodes and shorts. But if you are interested in learning more about writing for interactive stories and narrative games for the Web, you may want to check out *End-to-End Game Development* by Nick Iuppa and Terry Borst, *Digital Storytelling: A Creator's Guide For Interactive Entertainment, 2nd edition* by Carolyn Handler Miller, and *Game Design: From Blue Sky to Green Light* by Deborah Todd.

Democracy of the Web (well... at least for now).

The good news for interested writers is that writing for the Web (at least for the time being) is so much more democratic compared to writing for film, television and cable networks. There are fewer restrictions and limitations. Gone are the network/studio deals. Writers and creators can totally be their very own boss! There are no formal networks, and business is not conducted as it is in a traditional studio or network system, eliminating much of the confusing, off-putting, and ultimately frustrating "red tape."

In other words, there is no network or studio telling you that you cannot do another dysfunctional family comedy because they already have one on the air, another in development, and competing networks have two more family comedies also airing. If you feel your project is better than whatever else is on YouTube or any other Web channel, you can make it and post it out there to duke it out with any other family comedy Web offering to see if it can attract a loyal fan base. And, if you are fortunate enough, there could be the possibility that a sponsor will become a fan of your work and might offer to underwrite the cost of doing your series, which is exactly what happened for Scott Rice.

While there are some sponsors for the more popular Web series like *Script Cops, Prom Queen, Fred, LonelyGirl15, CTRL, The Bannen Way* and *Riese*, and while many of the network television series also sponsor websites with additional material related to their series, by and large, most of what you will see on YouTube and other Web channels is created, produced and posted by entrepreneurial writers and writer-directors like you, hoping that their series, sketches or shorts will catch fire and become the next hot Web sensation.

Admittedly, much of what we find on YouTube can fall into the categories of simply too-cute videos of pets and children, or rather amateurish "what-I-did-on-my-vacation" videologs. Nonetheless, the beauty of the Web is that everyone is allowed their expression of what they feel is entertainment, and the viewers can — in equally democratic fashion — readily click off or switch over to another site if the content does not entertain or appeal to them.

Creators are free to post just about anything they would like on the Web since, unlike television and cable networks, there is no Broadcast Standards and Practices or FCC (Federal Communications Commission, aka "Big Brother") to monitor the content of your program and fine you based on their criteria for inappropriate subject matter. Of course, that can be a negative factor of the Web, especially if you are a parent who has under-aged and impressionable children who may inadvertently (or not!) stumble upon some of the websites that are not appropriate.

But among the millions of postings there have been some real gems that have gained a legion of viewers and whose creators have gained sponsorship and recognition for their work. Initially, a majority of these successful creators had to use their own money and most had to rely on help from their friends and family to get started, but were delighted to find it much easier to get their work viewed on the Web rather than going through the traditional, multilayered submission process of the networks and studios.

We don't need no stinkin' agents... or managers... or distributors! (With sincere apologies to my friends who work in those areas.)

Another seemingly insurmountable barrier that is traditionally faced by screenwriters of film, cable and television, is obtaining an agent, entertainment attorney or manager to represent them so that they can circulate your work and put your material and your name out there for various writing assignments. Well, the good news is that Web writers/creators do not need agents or managers to do this since anyone who has the time, money and creative vision to put up a Web program or series can do so directly. Also, unlike in film or television, an unproduced writer does not need to have a sponsor-approved, name showrunner or an A-list director or attached prominent acting talent to get a project approved and greenlighted, so the process of "packaging" is absolutely not necessary — which means that on the Web, there is no real need for an agent, entertainment attorney, manager or distributor!

If your goal is to eventually break into writing or directing for film, one of the more positive by-products of having a successful Web series, short or program is that you can be sure that agents, managers and studio execs will take notice of you, and will probably contact you about moving your talents from the Web to the more traditional platform of film and television!

Writing for the Web vs. Writing for television.

When it comes to writing for a Web series or program, there are some distinct differences and limitations compared to writing for a conventional television or cable series.

According to Michael Ajakwe, the biggest limitation of all in writing for the Web is time. "You don't have as much (time) when you write for the Web, so you have to get into your story immediately." Carolyn Miller agrees, commenting, "Most Web content is made for 'snack sized' consumption — in other words, made to be enjoyed in a short period of time."

Some screenwriters are under the impression that writing for the Web should be a lot easier than writing for television or cable. After all, a majority of Web content can be shown and enjoyed in ten minutes or less. But as most professional writers will quickly confirm, it is infinitely easier to write long than short. The shorter the time frame, the more skilled you must be as a writer. Your writing is forced to be much tighter, and much more precise. There is less time for you to set up your premise, to develop your characters, and to still present a compelling and entertaining storyline. Many writers have tried writing for the Web and failed miserably, mistaken in the belief that all they had to do was simply squeeze a traditional half-hour television comedy into six or eight minutes.

"The Web audience has a much shorter attention span," comments Laurie Scheer, who teaches a popular online class (*Writing Scripts for Online Videos* for *MediaBistro.com*). "Anyone who wants to write Web content has to understand that the Web audience wants convenience… they want everything in short bites or segments."

In spite of the shorter time span for a webisode or Web short in comparison to a television or cable episode, the basic three-act structure is still the most applicable storytelling foundation. Each webisode must have the following:

> A beginning (set-up).

> A middle (conflict or challenge).

> An end (in a comedy, it is usually a humorous resolution to a discussion or situation; in a drama it is generally a cliffhanger designed to have the viewer return for the next installment).

It is important to remember that the Web audience wants to forget where they are and wants to be taken somewhere, even if it is just for that small amount of time while watching a webisode or short. Both Ajakwe and Scheer agree that having a solid storytelling structure is essentially what separates a successful Web series or Web program from being no more than simply random video.

And just as a weekly television or cable series relies heavily on strong character development and interaction to keep their audience coming back each and every week, having interesting characters with a unique, quirky or outrageous point of view is every bit as important to a Web short, and especially in a Web series over the course of a season.

The average television or cable series is anywhere from as few as twelve to as many as twenty-six episodes per season. Whereas in a Web series, a season is usually between eight to twelve episodes, although there have been instances when there have been as few as three episodes to as many as fifty episodes.

The length of an average comedic webisode is usually less than six minutes, compared to thirty minutes for a comedy series on television or cable. The length of an average dramatic webisode is usually from eight to ten minutes, which is far shorter than the length of an episode of a one-hour dramatic television series.

Needless to say, trying to do a television series like *Lost* — with its large cast of rotating characters — would not make it an ideal candidate for a Web series. Having a viable Web series or program all boils down to having a small group of very distinct characters and giving them something that's entertaining and relatable to express in a very short span of time.

Web shorts are usually in the five- to twelve-minute range, with the average being around eight to ten minutes in length. Comedic Web sketches like *Script Cops* usually hover closer to the five-minute mark.

Not counting reality or game/competition shows, when it comes to popular genres, network television/cable series are fairly evenly divided up between comedies and dramas. However, an interesting observation about Web series is that an overwhelming number of them seem to be comedies. One "guesstimate" is that roughly 80% of the Web series or shorts are comedies and only about 10% are dramas. The other 10% are divided amongst Vlogs, talk shows, travel, health, lifestyle or documentary-type presentations.

Michael Ajakwe points out that, in general, comedies tend to be much less expensive and time-consuming to stage and shoot than dramatic Web series. And that most comedy projects take up much less time to set up a storyline compared to setting up a storyline for drama. It is also interesting to note that some of the more successful and popular Web channels being viewed are devoted entirely to comedy, some of them in sketch format. *College Humor, Fred, Brevity TV, Rowdy Orbit,* and *Funny Or Die* are just a few of the most-viewed Web channels specializing in humor.

Given the limitation of time and budget, most Web series are usually restricted to no more than one or two scenes per webisode. It is not uncommon to see a majority of a webisode shot indoors — in a house, an office, a café, a dorm room, or a classroom. Or if a Web series or program is shot outdoors, it might be shot in a public park, a backyard, or on a beach or some other public place. Generally speaking, you will not be seeing large crowds of people, complex action scenes or vast battle sequences in a Web series.

While most Web content is live-action (possibly as much as 95%), there seems to be more animated series and shorts springing up on the Web radar. Some of the more visible animated Web series include *How It Should Have Ended*, *Happy Tree Friends*, and the award-winning *Orlando's Joint*.

Another big difference between the Web and television/cable is the budget. Shooting a series for the Web is so much less expensive and less complicated than trying to launch a series on a television of cable network. A typical television episode can be anywhere from $1.5-million to $5-million or more. Conventional television series like *Lost* or *24* are rumored to far exceed the $5-million per episode mark.

Some webisodes or Web shorts have been shot for little or no money. Laurie Scheer relays the story of the Web series *IKEA Heights*, in which an enterprising young filmmaker started covertly shooting his series in an IKEA store in Burbank, California, because it had all the settings for bedrooms, living rooms, kitchens and dining rooms. In the background of each webisode you can see real IKEA customers shopping for furniture. Eventually IKEA caught on, but, surprisingly, allowed the Canadian writer-director to get his shots in as long as it did not disrupt any customers or sales personnel. Needless to say, this is probably a huge exception to the rule, as most places of business aren't quite as understanding.

The cost of a webisode or program depends on how many setups you have, the type of locale, how many actors, how much crew is needed, and your postproduction needs. If you are fortunate enough to have attracted a sponsor, some have been known to allot anywhere from $3,500 to $5,000 per webisode, although that figure fluctuates depending on the sponsor and the Web project that is under consideration.

Where do I start?

Both Terry Borst and Carolyn Miller feel strongly that in order to create for the Web, you have to watch a lot of different kinds of Web content — both good and bad — before deciding what kind of Web series or program you would like to create. As is the case with writing for television, film or cable, watching television/cable series or theatrical movies is important to get a feel for what works and what does not work.

In particular, in watching webisodes or shorts, you will notice that the more successful shows have their own unique pacing and rhythm, and that needs to be recognized and respected. Web programs posted that exceed ten to twelve minutes seem to have noticeably less traffic and usually not many sponsors, if any at all.

Laurie Scheer suggests that if a writer wants to create something for the Web, they need to look for something that has not been on television or cable. "They should ask themselves: What isn't out there? What voice hasn't yet been served or heard?" She also suggests that writers look at as many Web series as possible to understand their "device"' or "hooks." As an example, Scheer uses a Web series called *Sam Has 7 Friends*. The device that hooks in the viewer is that over the course of the next eight episodes, we will learn that one of Sam's friends is going to try and kill her.

Once you have a project in mind, Scott Rice feels the best way to proceed is to come up with a **proof of concept**, which essentially means you need to shoot an episode or short on spec. In addition to shooting a spec project, you should also be prepared with a proposal to accompany your spec. The proposal should contain an overview of your Web series or program, a budget, plus information on you and your crew. In addition, you might want to arm yourself with a short synopsis of each episode in the first season.

What to do if you're not a trust-fund baby.

While the Web is pretty democratic, the reality is that unless you are a trust-fund baby, you will inevitably need funds to start shooting your Web program or series. Nearly all of the creators of the Web content you see had to start from ground zero — they had to tighten their belts, save as much as they could, and sometimes turn to friends and family for loans. Maxing out credit cards or mortgaging one's house may not necessarily be the best option, but here are some strategies that have worked for others.

Anyone who is funding their own project needs to think economically. Web creators often rely on friends and family to help them secure locations, volunteer as crew or cast, or use their connections to secure "in-kind" services in exchange for screen credit.

Carolyn Miller points out that YouTube has a partners' program that has produced a major income stream for a number of Web content writers. Scott Rice adds that in addition to YouTube, competing Web channel MySpace also has a similar partners' program worth looking into.

"Pursue product placement," suggests Laurie Scheer. "Ask a local clothing boutique or store if they would be willing to donate a shooting locale or wardrobe in exchange for an end credit. You'd be surprised how many local businesses are willing to help out, which, in turn, brings down the costs." Along the same line of thinking, consider asking if you can shoot in a location after hours so it will not disrupt business. I have heard that owners of some small, local restaurants have even thrown in some free food for a chance to be an extra in the background and for a screen credit for their business.

One enterprising writer-director even announced on his Facebook account that he needed actors within 100 miles of his location who would be willing to work for food, but no money. His Facebook account was swamped with interested thespians. He ended up doing some of his auditions via webcam and selected his top picks. The runners-up got to be background extras.

On a more serious note, another option for obtaining funding can be found through a website called Kickstarter (*kickstarter.com*), which is a funding platform for filmmakers, artists, designers, inventors, nonprofits, writers and others needing funding for their projects or to start their small businesses. I have seen filmmakers who will list their funding goal, along with a few sentences describing their project. Each project is given a specific amount of time to raise their goal. Interested visitors to the site can make donations toward the project that appeals to them. Some filmmakers have funding levels — e.g., for a $100 donation you will receive screen credit at the end of the film; for $250, you will received a screen credit and crew T-shirt; for $500, you will receive screen credit, crew T-shirt and a DVD of the film, etc.

Getting your work out there.

Because there are no agents or managers to circulate your work, you will be responsible for marketing your own projects.

Once Scott Rice finished postproduction on *Script Cops*, he posted it on ScottRiceFilms.com and told his friends, students, family and filmmaking contacts about it and got things going through word of mouth. A former student saw the first five episodes that Scott had made and mentioned it to an exec at Sony's Web content division and they viewed his proof of concept, along with his proposal, episode synopses and crew bios. The result is that they offered him a deal to do nine more webisodes as his sponsor.

Michael Ajakwe decided to take things one step further — he actually started his very own Web channel. He conferred with the designer of his website and realized that the difference in upgrading his site to a "channel" was a worthwhile investment. He already has his Web comedy *Who...* up on AjakweTV.com, with two more new series to follow close behind. All three of the series are his own creation and were written and directed by him. He said that having his own Internet channel allowed him to play Network Chief, so he could decide what makes the schedule and what gets cancelled. Already a noted television writer, having his own Internet channel also allowed him to diversify his brand as a creator/writer/producer by avoiding the limitations that the television and film industry often places on writers/creators.

In his own words, "On AjakweTV.com, there are no limits to what I can write and create and share with the public, and that pleases me immensely." Ajakwe already has some local sponsors, and interested fans are encouraged to donate a small fee to view three webisodes. He's confident that he will break even next year.

According to Carolyn Miller, "The Web is a little bit like the Wild West. You need a sense of adventure to succeed here." She also adds, "You can post your work on YouTube or on your own website and find an audience for it. Furthermore, there are even business models that you can employ to earn money from the material you create."

In addition to YouTube and MySpace, here are some other Web channels to consider, should you decide not to post your work on your own website or to create your own Web channel. Just keep in mind that since some of these companies are divisions of larger corporations, there may be restrictions or policies when it comes to submissions:

> **Atom.com** — Atom is a division of MTV and partners with Comedy Central.

> **Crackle.com** — Crackle is the Web content division of Sony

> **FunnyOrDie.com** — This site was started by Gary Sanchez Productions (Will Farrell is one of the partners) and features comedic content.

> **Babelgum.com** — An international site which also features an online film festival to showcase outstanding Web content.

> **CollegeHumor.com** — Started in 1999, this is one of the longer-running Web channels specializing in comedic content.

Now that I've posted my work, what's next?

Just as typing the last "FADE OUT" on a screenplay or teleplay is not really all a screenwriter has to do to get noticed, posting your short or Web series on the Internet is not all you have to do if you want to move ahead. It is important to think of you and your work as a product, and like all products, marketing is an absolute essential.

"Marketing means doing a lot of networking. It means getting the word out to all your contacts and not being afraid to make new contacts and to form a community," advises Scott Rice. "It means moving out of your comfort zone and submitting your shorts to film festivals and getting to know other filmmakers who are also attending."

Consider creating a Facebook account for your Web program and get your friends and family to tell their friends and family to become fans of your show. Getting the word out on Twitter is also another useful tool for letting others know about your program. If you submitted your short to a film festival, do not be shy about using Facebook and Twitter to let people know what day, date, location, and time your project will be featured.

In order to bring more attention to the creativity on the Web and to recognize some of the more outstanding Web material, Michael Ajakwe organized the Los Angeles Web Festival, which he calls LAWEBFEST (*lawebfest.com*). In its premiere outing, LAWEBFEST had more than 2,400 attendees, screened nearly fifty Web series, and awarded actor/writer/director Robert Townsend Web Series of the Year for *Diary of a Single Mom*. In addition, Ajakwe had workshops and panels on everything from creating/writing for the Web, how to get your own Web channel up and running, and how to make the connections you need to succeed.

It is encouraging to know that Web festivals are being enthusiastically formed in the United States and Canada as well in Europe and Asia. Entering your Web series or short in a festival and taking the time to meet and greet other Web entrepreneurs who are attending can only increase your contact base and add validity to your name and your work. Scott Rice points out that "Many film festivals have a category for shorts and it doesn't matter if it's a theatrical short or one made specifically for the Web." And let's not forget that producers, agents and studio/television execs also attend film festivals, making this kind of an event fertile ground for networking as well as for having an opportunity to have your project shown to others.

Laurie Scheer is quick to add that because change comes so quickly, writers must keep up to date on everything that is going on with the Web. One of her daily "must-dos" is checking out Cynthia Turner's Cynopsis Media website (*cynopsis.com*) for the latest breaking news on what is happening on the Webfront — new Web channels, exciting new websites, mergers, alliances, deals, updates, etc. She considers reading Cynopsis Media Digital as essential as the industry trades *The Hollywood Reporter* and *Variety*.

Can writing for the Web lead to writing for television/film?

According to Michael Ajakwe, writing for the Web is a great way to break into film and television "because it shows what you can do — not just as a writer, but as a producer. It proves you can come up with an idea and actually execute it. That has value. Nobody wants to read in Hollywood, so if they can go online and watch what you've done in five or ten minutes, that's a good thing. Plus, as we've heard from the beginning of time, a picture is worth a thousand words."

Laurie Scheer readily concurs, "Once you have a Web series or short and have gained a following, you can use it as 'proof' that you can take an idea and run with it. You can direct a network or studio exec to the Web to view your work, or you can send them a DVD. It's the same thing as having an old-fashioned 'promo reel' that shows them what you are really capable of. In addition, the WGA recognizes writers of Web content, which means there are crossover opportunities."

As an example of how writing for the Web can lead to writing for film, cable or television, here is a true story from a colleague of mine who used to work at one of the major networks:

One proactive intern who was working at the network enthusiastically volunteered to spend a few hours on updating the website of a popular network television show. Every day the intern would diligently read all the comments and questions on the website from fans. With the permission of the showrunner and the network, the intern started a discussion group. He would post an intriguing question or topic that had to do with either a key storyline on the series or an important character of the show each day. In a few short weeks, traffic on the show's website had jumped three-fold. He realized that many of the responders were female and they seemed to be taking quite an interest in one of the secondary male characters. Noting this, the intern talked to the supervising producer and suggested that a blog be written once a week from the point of view of that particular male character, and he volunteered to write the blog. As a result of the thousands of daily hits each week, the network quickly recognized that the "**TV-Q**" (popularity quotient) of that character deserved more exposure. The enterprising intern gave the showrunner and supervising producer an episodic premise he had written which, coincidentally, prominently featured the character, and he was allowed to write the episode under the watchful eye of one of the story editors. As the series started featuring that character more often, the Nielsen ratings started to rise. None of this would have happened if the intern had not used the show's website to increase interest in the series — which is where he is now happily working full-time on the writing staff.

If you are a fan of a particular television show, you may want to send a query letter to someone on the writing staff to see if they are considering adding on more story or character background information on the show's website. It is not uncommon for some of the series to have behind-the-scenes stories, blogs or journals supposedly being written by one or two of the main characters, or even a villain, of the series. Occasionally, writing assistants are assigned to write the blogs or journal entries, but writing assistants are also very eager to be promoted to staff writing positions, and when they do, someone will have to take their place and it has to be someone who is already familiar with the series and all of its characters. While you may not get a public writing credit for writing material for a television show's website, it usually is a paid position as well as one way of gaining some valuable experience as a writer, not to mention an excellent opportunity to gain those much-needed contacts for your writing career. Also, this specific kind of writing assignment gives you a better idea on whether or not you would enjoy writing for the Web or writing for television.

One writer-director of a popular Web series recently had Hollywood knocking on his door with an offer to direct a dark, offbeat teen comedy which had a major up-and-coming young male star attached. While the writer-director ultimately turned down this offer (because he really felt the tone of the story was too dark for his sensibility), the big Tinseltown producer is such a huge fan of his that I have no doubt that it will not be too long before this talented Web content creator will have another opportunity to transition from cyberspace to the big screen.

Another example of how writing for the Web can open doors to television or cable: One of the more prominent Web series that has been acquired for the cable venue Showtime is *Web Therapy*, which was co-written/produced by and stars actress Lisa Kudrow of *Friends* fame. Each webisode is about three minutes long, which is exactly how long her character, therapist Fiona, feels each Web therapy session with her annoying clients should last.

And several comedic sketch series featured on the *Funny Or Die* Web channel have been given a new home at cable giant HBO, which is further proof that writing for the Web is yet another viable plank in multi-platforming!

Food for thought.

Let's face it, writing for the Web may not be everyone's cup of chai, but we all have to admit that within the last decade, the Internet has certainly made an indelible impression on everyone's life and has become a new form of media that cannot be ignored and deserves to be respected.

Carolyn Miller notes, "You need a sense of adventure to succeed here... However, it is an exciting area for writers who are entrepreneurial enough to produce their own material, either alone or with a group of colleagues."

"Anyone can get in. Anyone — from anywhere — provided you have a camera, a computer and some talent. It gives people who don't have the opportunity or resources to make films or a TV show a chance to express themselves and reach potentially millions of people," adds Michael Ajakwe.

According to Laurie Scheer, "In the near future, the Web will be our primary form of communication. All you have to do is look around, and you'll notice that broadcasting is already headed in that direction."

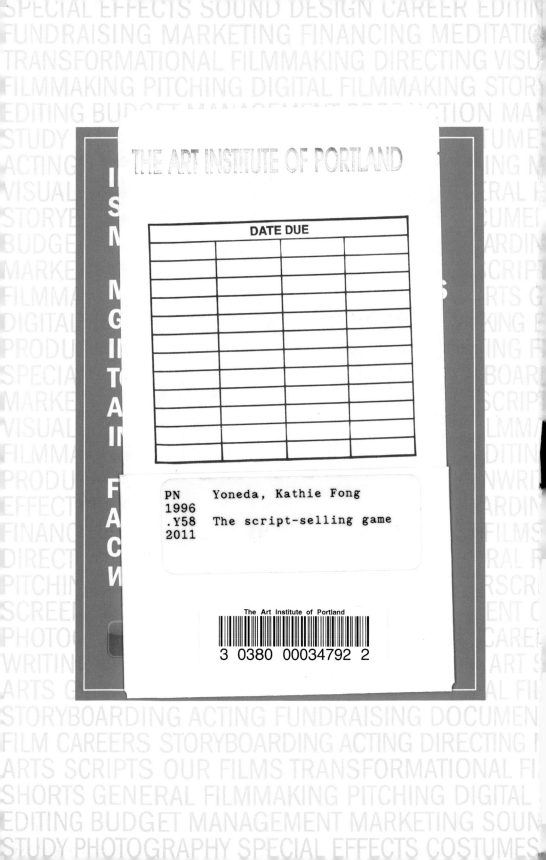

In a dark time, a light bringer came along, leading the curious and the frustrated to clarity and empowerment. It took the well-guarded secrets out of the hands of the few and made them available to all. It spread a spirit of openness and creative freedom, and built a storehouse of knowledge dedicated to the betterment of the arts.

The essence of the Michael Wiese Productions (MWP) is empowering people who have the burning desire to express themselves creatively. We help them realize their dreams by putting the tools in their hands. We demystify the sometimes secretive worlds of screenwriting, directing, acting, producing, film financing, and other media crafts.

By doing so, we hope to bring forth a realization of 'conscious media' which we define as being positively charged, emphasizing hope and affirming positive values like trust, cooperation, self-empowerment, freedom, and love. Grounded in the deep roots of myth, it aims to be healing both for those who make the art and those who encounter it. It hopes to be transformative for people, opening doors to new possibilities and pulling back veils to reveal hidden worlds.

MWP has built a storehouse of knowledge unequaled in the world, for no other publisher has so many titles on the media arts. Please visit www.mwp.com where you will find many free resources and a 25% discount on our books. Sign up and become part of the wider creative community!

Onward and upward,

Michael Wiese
Publisher/Filmmaker

About Kathie Fong Yoneda

Photo by Peggy David

KATHIE FONG YONEDA has worked in film and television for more than thirty years. She has held executive positions at Disney, Touchstone, Disney TV Animation, Paramount Pictures Television, and Island Pictures, specializing in development and story analysis of both live-action and animation projects.

Kathie is an internationally known seminar leader on screenwriting and development and has conducted workshops in France, Germany, Austria, Spain, Ireland, Great Britain, Australia, Indonesia, Thailand, Singapore, and throughout the U.S. and Canada. She was a special guest of the Soviet Peace Committee for a symposium in Moscow and was selected Keynote Speaker for Asian-Pacific Heritage Month at the Smithsonian Institute. She is also on The Board of Directors for *IMAGO*, a French film, television, and media company.

In addition to her solo workshops, Kathie also team-teaches with screenwriting author/consultant Dr. Linda Seger, producer and Academy-Award winning writer Pamela Wallace (*Witness*), and author/mythologist/consultant Pamela Jaye Smith. She also is a faculty member of Writers University, where she teaches an online class on *Pitch and Presentation*.

Kathie was co-executive producer on the cable network teen series *Beyond the Break*, and has been published in *The Portable Writers Conference* and *Writers Aide*, and has been interviewed for dozens of magazines, trade papers, newspapers, e-zines, websites, radio, blogs, and television.

Kathie lives in central California with her husband, Dennis, and enjoys traveling, reading and cooking.

For story consultations and workshops/speaking engagements, please visit Kathie's website at *kathiefongyoneda.com*, or follow Kathie on Facebook.

A Few Last Words

In my career, I have had the wonderful opportunity to meet and work with thousands of writers. Some have won Oscars and Emmys, while many others were just starting on their very first script. One thing most of these people had in common was an insatiable compulsion to put words to paper with the hope of seeing those words committed to film. And whether their latest script sold or was rejected, the writers who ultimately succeeded or continued to work were those who just could not stop writing.

Some might view these people as obsessed, but I beg to differ. True writers cannot help themselves. They are driven to write. And although writer's block does come along every once in a while, for the most part writers cannot stop the ideas and the words from flowing — and, we, the moviegoing public, are the fortunate beneficiaries of their creative insanity!

And this second time around, I would like to recognize that writers (myself included) cannot do it all alone — so I want to pay special thanks to the families and friends of writers everywhere who believe in their loved one's creative dreams and continue to smile every time they come up with yet another terrific idea for a feature film, Web or television project. Your love and patience are what keeps all of us writers going!

To all of the wonderful writers I have worked with — past, present and future — thank you for inspiring me with your creativity and empowering the world with your words!